CANOEING AND KAYAKING COLLEGE CAMPUSES IN MICHIGAN

DOC FLETCHER

authorHOUSE®

AuthorHouse™
1663 Liberty Drive
Bloomington, IN 47403
www.authorhouse.com
Phone: 1 (800) 839-8640

www.canoeingmichiganrivers.com

Photographs: Doc Fletcher except Steve Arnosky (Clinton River chapter 3rd photo)
and Chris Wall/Heavner Nature Connection (Rouge River 1st photo)
Maps: Maggie Meeker

Published by AuthorHouse 02/12/2016

ISBN: 978-1-5049-7941-2 (sc)
ISBN: 978-1-5049-7942-9 (e)

Library of Congress Control Number: 2016902396

Print information available on the last page.

Table of Contents

The Introduction to Canoeing and Kayaking College Campuses

The great philosopher Bluto Blutarsky once said, *"7 years of college down the drain – might as well join the (expletive deleted) Peace Corps"*. No Bluto, that's not the way to look at it. College is such an incredible experience that stretching the adventure out a few years seems very sensible AND if you're fortunate enough to attend an institution that has a river meandering through or nearby, well, that's about as good as good gets.

With a Michigan map spread across the desk and a bit of time spent researching colleges across the Great Lakes State, it is evident that there are over 20 Michigan colleges that can tell you they have a great paddling river for a neighbor. 20 of those college-river unions are highlighted in this book.

The rivers written about were paddled with a GPS, a waterproof camera, and a digital voice recorder. Utilizing these 3 items on the water allowed me to measure miles & minutes from start to finish and from start to key landmarks along the way (and inform readers about what to expect on the journey, and how far each landmark is from the river launch), plus photograph and communicate the beauty of the river and its surroundings.

Whatever your age, canoeing or kayaking all 20 river trips in this book will earn you a *Degree in Riverology*:

In the Upper Peninsula, Michigan Tech Huskies (Houghton) and Keweenaw Peninsula residents & visitors can relax with a paddle down the Bete Grise (*bay-da greez*) River, while Northern Michigan Wildcats (Marquette) can take a study break with their friends 'n fellow travelers by paddling the nearby Escanaba River. In the Lower Peninsula, there's a long list of recreational paddling opportunities in collegiate backyards...

Boardman River@ Northwestern Michigan College (Traverse City) Chippewa River @ Central Michigan University (Mount Pleasant) Clinton River @ Oakland University (Rochester) Flint River @ University of Michigan Flint (Flint) Grand River @ Grand Valley State University (Allendale) Grand River @ Jackson College (Jackson) Huron River @ Eastern Michigan University (Ypsilanti) Huron River @ University of Michigan (Ann Arbor) Kalamazoo River @ Albion College (Albion) Kalamazoo River @ Western Michigan University (Kalamazoo) Kawkawlin River @ Saginaw Valley State University (University Center/Saginaw) Macatawa (Black) River @ Hope College (Holland) Muskegon River @ Ferris State University (Big Rapids) (not that) Pine River @ Alma College (Alma) Red Cedar River @ Michigan State University (East Lansing) Rouge River (Lower & Middle Branch) @ University of Michigan Dearborn (Dearborn) Thunder Bay River @ Alpena Community College (Alpena) Tittabawassee River @ Northwood University (Midland)

Each river gets its own chapter that includes...

- The river's *Degree of Paddling Difficulty*, a simple 3 level assessment: beginner (1), intermediate (2), and (the most difficult) skilled (3);

- *The Livery contact* to service your trip on the river, which will include canoe/kayak rental, (ask for availability of) car spotting & hauling, and the livery's expert advice on how the river is running that day;

- *Local Detroit Tiger radio station*, so you can follow the Boys of Summer while away from home;

- *Directions* to the launch site and the take-out;

- *Background of the River* including its length, flow direction, occasional historical tidbits, and environmental stewards of the river;

- *Camping* near the river;

- *Paddling the River* gives minutes and miles from launch to take-out and from launch to interesting landmarks along the journey;

- *The College* fun facts, brief history, and what makes that institute unique;

- *The Tavern* near campus to kick back at after a day on the water and grab a fine bar burger or other good grub and to wet your whistle.

Re-live the magic of those crazy college days via a 3-part curriculum... (1) paddle the river, (2) walk the nearby college campus & (3) enjoy the local tavern. College, for many the greatest experience of our lives... expanding minds, no parents, first taste of independence, learning responsibility, building life-long friendships, and – like the joy of paddling a river - creating a long list of happy, fantastic memories.

Having fun is important, but safety is always the #1 priority, so... never paddle alone, wear your life vest, and always call the livery for the latest river conditions before you head out on the water.

Streaming Higher Education Your Way, Doc Fletcher

Dedication

To the memory of my Mom and Dad,
Mary Louise and Herbert Roy Fletcher,
for sending me off to college and
for immersing me into the waters.

To Betty Jane Harlow,
for introducing me and so many others
for over 4 decades
to the beauty of the Looking Glass River;
rest in peace my friend.

Acknowledgments

To Maggie, my bride of 35 years. *What could make me feel this way?* My Girl.

To my family for their love and sunshine.

To my friends for being spiritual brothers and sisters.

To Carl "Doubles" Verba for suggesting the theme of this book as we paddled the Huron River.

To the Crack Research Team, my compadres on the rivers, for sharing their knowledge, insights, humor, songs, stories, snacks, and love.

To the canoe and kayak livery owners in Michigan, for always putting safety number 1, for their passion in getting folks out on the rivers, and for doing the heavy lifting in keeping the waters free of debris as much as possible for our recreational paddling fun.

To the environmental and paddling groups throughout the state, and their time and effort in restoring/maintaining the health and beauty of our waters. You are a true blessing to Michigan.

To fellow paddlers visited at the Quiet Water Symposium and at libraries across Michigan, for attending my talks and sharing their river stories and love of the waters.

To Michigan's colleges and universities for the experiences offered and the wisdom they impart (*"Knowledge is Good"* – Emil Faber), with special thanks to my alma mater, Eastern Michigan University, where I met Maggie on my 20th birthday and Chucky my first day on campus: Once a Huron, Always a Huron.

To Michigan's tavern owners for the great bar burgers, Pabst on tap, and keeping the lights on.

To Frank Lary for whupping the New York Yankees on a regular basis (28 and 13) and to Norm Cash for a career of bringing happiness to Detroit Tiger fans (number 25 forever).

To God for the incredible blessings He has bestowed upon me, and for allowing me to live my life in Michigan.

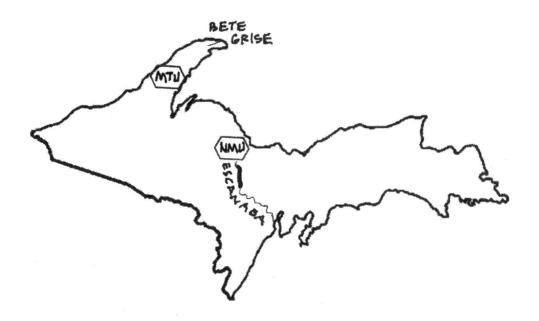

The rivers and the colleges:

Bete Grise River / MTU-Michigan Tech University (Houghton)

Boardman River / NMC-Northwestern Michigan College (Traverse City)

Chippewa River / CMU-Central Michigan University (Mount Pleasant)

Clinton River / OU-Oakland University (Rochester)

Escanaba River / NMU-Northern Michigan University (Marquette)

Flint River / UMF-University of Michigan Flint (Flint)

Grand River / GVSU-Grand Valley State University (Allendale)

Grand River / JC-Jackson College (Jackson)

Huron River / EMU-Eastern Michigan University (Ypsilanti)

Huron River / UM-University of Michigan (Ann Arbor)

Kalamazoo River / AC-Albion College (Albion)

Kalamazoo River / WMU-Western Michigan University (Kalamazoo)

Kawkawlin River / SVSU-Saginaw Valley State University (University Center/Saginaw)

Macatawa (Black) River / HC-Hope College (Holland)

Muskegon River / FSU-Ferris State University (Big Rapids)

(not that) Pine River / AC-Alma College (Alma)

Red Cedar River / MSU-Michigan State University (East Lansing)

Rouge River (Lower & Middle Br.) / UMD-University of Michigan Dearborn (Dearborn)

Thunder Bay River / ACC-Alpena Community College (Alpena)

Tittabawassee River / NU-Northwood University (Midland)

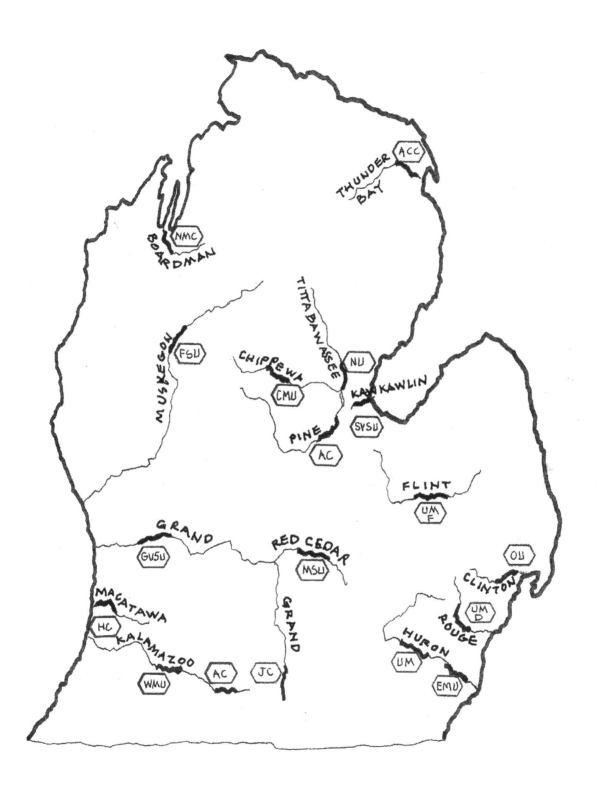

Bete Grise River/ Michigan Tech University

Degree of Paddling Difficulty: skilled (level 3 of 3) the first half-mile when the Lake Superior shoreline can be choppy and wind-driven at times; beginner (1 of 3) the balance of the trip.

Livery: Keweenaw Adventure Company, 155 Gratiot Street, Copper Harbor MI 49918; (906) 289-4303; www.keweenawadventure.com. The livery offers hauling and car spotting services.

River Quote: "Doc, stop lap-stroking" – John Parsons (my stern-man Johnny telling me to set down my camera and digital recorder, pick up the paddle from my lap, and do some actual paddling)

Bete Grise Soundtrack: Without the River – Squeaky Clean Cretins (Danny's song), Swing That Thing – Luke Winslow-King Band, Lara Jones – Divino Nino, Bohemian Groove – the Macpodz, No Beer – Michigan Tech Husky Pep Band

Detroit Tigers radio stations: listen to WCCY 1400AM or 99.3FM to follow the Tigers when paddling the Bete Grise near the Michigan Tech campus.

Directions to the launch site: from Houghton, take 41 North to Gay Lac La Belle Road and turn right. Follow Gay Lac La Belle Road past Mount Bohemia to the town of Lac La Belle (French for "Lake Beautiful"). Turn left on to Lac La Belle Road/Bete Grise Road and drive to Bete Grise Bay.

Directions to the take-out: same as the launch site. No restrooms at launch/take-out.

Background of the Bete Grise River:

Pronounced *bay-da greez* by many locals, the Bete Grise River is only a mile long, but it is a gateway to beauty well beyond its dimensions. Bete Grise River & Bay and the town of Bete Grise are located in the Upper Peninsula's Keweenaw Peninsula, just southwest of Copper Harbor. The river and the bay lie within the Bete Grise Preserve, part of 1,800 acres of dune swale wetlands (swale meaning the valley or low lying place along/between the dunes) and 7,500' of protected shoreline at Lake Superior. One of the Preserve's champions is the *Stewards of Bete Grise Preserve*, working to generate education/appreciation/protection of the BGP. Follow their efforts at www. betegrisepreserve.org/Stewards_of_Bete_Grise_Preserve/Home.html.

Within the Keweenaw Peninsula that Michigan Tech calls home, it can arguably be said that no river offers a more fascinating experience than the Bete Grise River. This trip takes you to the white sand beaches of Lake Superior at Bete Grise Bay, by the

Mendota Lighthouse, alongside dunes and wetlands, into lovely Lac La Belle (French for "beautiful lake"), offers fantastic views of Mount Bohemia, all while sharing the space with eagles and sandhill cranes. The fishing is outstanding for smallmouth bass, perch, pike, walleye, lake trout and, in the fall, salmon. Trees populating the Preserve include white pine, cedar, tamarack, and spruce.

Camping: Lake Fanny Hooe Resort and Campground, 505 Second Street, Copper Harbor MI 49918; (906) 289-4451; www.fannyhooe.com. A trout stream flows through this wooded campground, with sites ranging from rustic to full service campsites. All sites have water, electric (30 amps), a picnic table and a fire pit. Full service sites also include sewer and cable TV. Amenities include a dump station, hot showers, and bathrooms.

Paddling the Bete Grise River:

Journeying through the Bete Grise Preserve offers a wide variety of paddling routes through the river and the interlocking lagoons. Outlined below is only one option, paddled in July...

- Total trip 3.5 miles, 1 hour & 35 minutes (river/lagoons offer day-long paddling options)

Launch on Bete Grise Bay at Lake Superior's public beach (near picnic tables and restrooms) and turn right/south. Paddle for 1/2 mile until reaching the channel and turn right/west, passing between the metal-braced channel walls. The channel is dredged as needed by the Army Corps of Engineers, maintaining a sufficient depth (20' est.) to allow it to act as a "harbor of refuge" for small freighters seeking temporary shelter from Lake Superior's storms.

.7 mile/20 minutes: after paddling through the metal channel walls, and seeing Lac La Belle (lake) directly ahead, turn down the first body of water to your right/north – Bete Grise River. Although called a river, the Bete Grise River differs little from the grouping of lagoons and backwaters you've just paddled into.

A 3-member family of sandhill cranes is 10' beyond the riverbank, and they allow us to get within 20' of them.

1.1 miles/30 minutes: turn around at the right bend by the boathouse also on the right, and head south, back towards the channel.

1.5 miles/38 minutes: reaching the channel you face the Mendota Lighthouse, today a private residence. Departing the river, turn right/west on the channel and paddle towards Lac La Belle.

1.6 miles/40 minutes: turn right/north into the next lagoon. A bald eagle flies over the canoe and kayak group, a common sight in this area.

1.8 miles/46 minutes: reach the northern end of the lagoon; follow it as it bends to the left and, clearly visible ahead and to the right (i.e. to the northwest) is beautiful

Mount Bohemia. Mount Bohemia features the steepest ski run in the Midwest, with the greatest vertical drop (900') and the deepest powder.

2 miles/51 minutes: having followed the bend in the lagoon, you are back at the channel; Lac La Belle is only 1/5th of a mile to the right/west. Do not turn towards Lac La Belle, instead stay on a southern line, cross over the channel and into another lagoon.

2.3 miles/1 hour: paddle into the lagoon as far as you can into the far left/south corner, where the "Bete Grise Preserve" sign is on a beach, a fine place to pull the boats ashore and take a break. From the Preserve sign, paddle to the right and back towards the channel (an option is to paddle to the left and into Lac La Belle).

2.6 miles/1 hour and 8 minutes: once back at the channel, turn right/east towards Lake Superior.

3 miles/1 hour and 20 minutes: after passing back through the channel's metal walls, you are on the shores of Lake Superior – turn left/north and paddle along the shoreline.

3.5 miles/1 hours and 35 minutes: you're in! having reached the picnic tables and restrooms at the white sands of the Bete Grise Bay public beach.

Bete Grise River Crack Research Team: John Parsons, Yoshi Schlager, Carl Hayden, Seiko, Doc

The College: Michigan Technological University

1400 Townsend Drive, Houghton, MI 49931, phone 906-487-1885; www.mtu.edu.

Michigan Technological University, popularity known as Michigan Tech, was founded in 1885. Its original name was the Michigan Mining School, reflecting its mission as a training grounds for mining engineers, until renamed the Michigan College of Mining and Technology in 1925. Why mining? Before the California Gold Rush of 1849, there was the Keweenaw Peninsula Copper Rush of 1843. As there were no roads, the mining rush came by boat through the town named Copper Harbor (just minutes from the Bete Grise River) and the Keweenaw was on its way to becoming a major industrial mining center.

By the time this institute of higher learning had its name changed to Michigan Technological University in 1964, the school's curriculum had broadened to include programs in physics, forestry, engineering administration, and chemical, electrical, civil, mechanical, & geological engineering.

The Keeweenaw Peninsula's Bete Grise River and its University both are smaller than most others listed in this book, but project well-beyond their size: while the tiny, picturesque Bete Grise River is a gateway to a more expansive area of beauty, so the cozy-community/ family-feel MTU has earned a place in the top tier of national universities according to, among others, US News & World Report. In a review of graduate level programs, US News & World Report includes 4 of MTU's in their USA's top 100: materials science and engineering as well as chemical, computer, & electrical engineering.

Of all the rankings and recognition received by Michigan Tech, perhaps the coolest is this one - 95 percent of MTU students have jobs in their chosen field, enroll in graduate school, or enlist in the military by the time they graduate. Not far behind, and maybe just as impressive, is the university's student-to-faculty ratio of 11 to 1.

A MTU point of emphasis is in teaching students to become citizens who contribute to the sustainability of our world. In 2011, the university initiated the "MOST" program, acronym for the Michigan Tech Open Sustainability Technology. MOST focus is on, to directly quote from the MTU website, "open and applied sustainability, which is the application of science and innovation to ensure a better quality of life for all, now and into the future, in a just and equitable manner, whilst living within the limits of supporting ecosystems".

Houghton, home to Michigan Tech, is a community featured in the guidebook, "The 100 Best Small Towns in America" (author Norman Crampton). Houghton sits on the south bank of the wide Portage River, across the water from the town of Hancock. Many views from the Portage riverbanks can be accurately described as spectacular, whatever the season, including winters that often yield snowfalls of over 200 inches. Each February, the annual Winter Carnival finds students participating in 3 days of snow-statue-building (including an all-night sculpting marathon), snow volleyball, ice bowling (in which a student becomes a human bowling ball), ice fishing, cross-country ski races, fireworks, and the Sno-Ball dance.

What better way to conclude a visit to the Michigan Tech campus then with a song by MTU mascot Blizzard T. Husky and the Husky Pep Band, the high energy group of musicians self-described as "The Cream of the Keeweenaw, The Pride of Pasty Land, The Second-Best Feeling in the World". Here are a few lines from their unique version of an old polka standard...

No Beer!

In Heaven there is no snow,
That's why we want to go.
And when it's ten below,
Our friends will be freezing in the snow.

In Heaven there are no refs,
But here they're blind and deaf.
And when we all have left,
Our friends will be BITCHIN' AT THE REFS.

The Tavern: Fitzgerald's Eagle River Inn, 5033 Front Street, Eagle River MI 49950; (906) 337-0666; www.eagleriverinn.com.

Fitzgerald's is extremely popular with Michigan Tech profs, hipsters, and beer snobs – but don't let that stop you from relaxing here after a day of paddling. Owners Mike 'n Marc are very accommodating, and the Lake Superior beachfront view from the deck is wonderful. "The Fitz" features over 100 craft beers, over 100 fine whiskeys and receives consistently sparkling reviews for their excellent food. After an evening of sampling, the rooms at the attached Inn make the perfect accompaniment. The bar, the dining area, and the rooms all face the beach. Nice.

The nearby town of Ahmeek presents the annual Farm Block Fest, 3 days of peace and music (thank you Max Yasgur) in late-July/early-August, a fundraiser providing instruments and music lessons for area youth. Musicians appearing in each Farm Block Fest are invited to perform at Fitzgerald's the night before the Fest, providing them with income that helps ensure the flow of top grade Fest performers annually.

Word on the river is that the smoker creations at the Fitz yield the finest BBQ in the North.

Chapter Sources: John Parsons, www.mtu.edu

Boardman River/ Northwestern Michigan College

Degree of Paddling Difficulty: beginner (level 1 of 3)

Livery: The River Traverse City, 161 E. Grandview Parkway (Clinch Park), Traverse City MI 49684; (231) 883-1413; www.231outfitters.com. The livery offers hauling and car spotting services.

River Quote: "Today was meant for canoe travel" – Dick Proenneke ("Alone in the Wilderness")

Boardman River Soundtrack: Take Me There (Traverse City) – Hacky Turtles, Wade in the Water – Ramsey Lewis Trio, Blue Skies – Oh Brother Big Sister, Light Blue – Bobby Darin, The River of No Return – Tex Williams

Detroit Tigers radio station: listen to WCCW 1310AM to follow the Tigers when paddling the Boardman through Traverse City.

Directions to the launch site: in downtown Traverse City, take Union Street south to 8th Street, turn left/east on to 8th Street. Follow 8th Street east to the Woodmere Library and turn right/south. Once past the library, turn right/west on to Hannah Avenue into Hull Park. The boat ramp will be on your left. Restrooms are available.

Directions to the take-out: in downtown Traverse City, take Grandview Parkway to Union Street, turn north on Union Street into Clinch Park. Follow the bend in the road to the brown shack of "The River". The boat ramp is next to the brown shack. Restrooms are available.

Background of the Boardman River:

The 26-mile journey of the Main Branch of the Boardman begins in the town of Kalkaska, at the merger of the river's North and South branches, a merger known as "the Fork". From the Fork, the Boardman flows southwest until it is directly south of Traverse City, where it begins to turn to the north, flowing through the land purchased by Captain Boardman in 1847, and on into the West Arm of Grand Traverse Bay. The river is known as one of Michigan's top 10 trout streams.

A peaceful and slow urban paddle best describes the beginner-friendly trip outlined in this chapter, launching (where the river widens) at Boardman Lake, then alongside homes and businesses on the way to Grand Traverse Bay. The Boardman flows faster upstream from this chapter's stretch, moving briskly and with spirit as the river floor drops 8' per mile through occasional white water, with the most aggressive rapids north of the Beitner Road Bridge.

The folks at the Traverse Area Paddle Club are a true blessing to those who love our waters. Begun in 1999 to bring paddlers together for social outings on the water, the TAPC has morphed into a first class environmental group, scheduling river clean-ups on not only the Boardman, but also on the Sturgeon, the Platte, the Jordan, the Betsie, and the Pine among their 120 river adventures annually. Their website is www. traverseareapaddleclub.org.

Also working to keep the Boardman pristine is the Chairman of the Board(man) himself, Norman R. Fred, and his group the BRCS, acronym for the Boardman River Clean Sweep. Frequently working in conjunction with the TAPC, you can check out Norm's schedule at www.brcleansweep.org.

"The River Traverse City" livery services the section of the Boardman River referenced in this chapter. In addition to rentals of kayaks, canoes, rafts, tubes, paddleboards, bicycles, and the fitness classes he offers, TRTC owner Mike Sutherland schedules "KaBrew" each Monday-Friday between 4-7PM (KaBrew = Kayaking + Brew Tour). The 3-hour KaBrew starts with a bike ride on the TART (Traverse Area Recreation and Transportation) Trail to brewery #1 and your first pint, then walk down the bluff to the kayak (or paddleboard) waiting for you and, after paddling to and stopping at several brew pubs or microbreweries along the way, arrive back at Clinch Park by 7PM. The River Traverse City works in tandem with each KaBrew pub to ensure the brew pubs staff enough people to properly wait on the 25-30 folks who arrive all at once on each kayak/paddleboard stop.

Camping: Traverse City State Park, 1132 US-31, Traverse City, MI 49686; (231) 922-5270. The state park resides east of downtown, across US31 from the East Arm of

Grand Traverse Bay, connected to the beach by a pedestrian bridge. The heavily wooded park has 350 campsites, 2 mini-cabins, and a 3-bedroom/2-bath cottage. *Fun option:* Northwestern Michigan College rents out rooms in their dorms including single rooms, double rooms, and family suites – and the use of bicycles is complimentary. Call the College at (231) 995-1000 for more information.

Paddling the Boardman:

- Total trip 2.4 miles, 1 hour and 5 minutes (check livery website for 2 hour trip option)

This paddle takes you through the urban section of the Boardman River, beginning in the northeast corner of Boardman Lake and providing you with the unique perspective of viewing the homes and businesses of downtown Traverse City from river level. To visualize today's trip, think of the river as a large "V" lying on its side, open end to the right/east and closed end to the left/west. Begin to canoe and kayak in a northwest direction until arriving at the bottom of the "V" at the Front Street Bridge, then making the big turn to the northeast, following the northeast line until the trip ends (the starting point is almost directly south of the take-out).

Launch at the Hull Park boat ramp next to the sailing school. There are restrooms at Hull Park. Upon launching from the boat ramp, you are facing south and treated to a view of a lake often full of sail boats. Paddle to the right, and in 5 minutes you will canoe and kayak beneath first a pedestrian bridge then a train trestle. There was plenty of deep water during our June trip as there is throughout the year.

.4 mile/13 minutes: paddle beneath the 8th Street Bridge. Along the sea wall, downstream from the 8th Street Bridge and on the left bank, are docked canoes, kayaks, and pontoon boats.

Unlike the Boardman River experience upstream from here, an enjoyable fast water run, the current through downtown is slow, perfect for allowing you plenty of time to take in all of the downtown activity, sights, and river side structures. This is a great little urban trip!

.7 mile/21 minutes: passing below the Cass Street Bridge, the Boardman dam emerges directly ahead.

A portage is required at the dam: paddle to the dirt path at the left of the dam. After a 150' walk, re-enter the river in the knee-deep water at the dock.

.8 mile/26 minutes: paddle beneath the Union Street Bridge. Brady's Bar (see "The Tavern" later in this chapter) is one block to your left.

1.2 miles/36 minutes: you're paddling under the Front Street Bridge. The popular and always busy section of Front Street runs to your right as you're at the extreme west end of the "V"-shaped river trip.

1.4 miles/41 minutes: once again, paddle below the Union Street Bridge, 4 blocks directly north of where you were 15 minutes ago. Here, the river trip briefly changes from urban to rural as you pass through a thick forest of trees and bushes along each river bank. Emerging from this short forest, you can see the back entrances to the stores on Front Street to your right.

1.5 miles/44 minutes: canoe and kayak below the Cass Street Bridge. Just past the bridge and to your left rises a cool looking sculpture – a metal robot holding a canoe. On the right, just a few store fronts apart, is the Mackinaw Brewing Company then the Grand Traverse Distillery as you're caught between a brew 'n a hard (liquor) place! A series of pedestrian bridges takes visitors over the river to the stores along Front Street.

1.6 miles/48 minutes: just past Horizon Books on the right, paddle beneath the Park Street Bridge.

1.9 miles/55 minutes: **what a gorgeous view of the bay** as you turn left/north and paddle under the Grandview Parkway Bridge. The flat water part of your trip now suddenly ends, as you enter the choppy waters of the West Arm of Grand Traverse

Bay. Once you clear the wall, turn left/west and paddle towards the brown shack and boat ramp, 10 minutes in the distance. The beach spreads out on your left.

2.4 miles/1 hour and 5 minutes: you're in! at the Clinch Park boat ramp, next to the brown shack of The River Traverse City livery.

Boardman River Crack Research Team: Sandy and J Jay Johnson, Maggie and Doc.

The College: Northwestern Michigan College

1701 E. Front Street, Traverse City, MI 49686, phone (231) 995-1000; www.nmc.edu.

Having a little fun with Northwestern Michigan College and Bob Seger... "I wanna be a lawyer, a doctor or professor, a member of the NMC... yeah". Although NMC is a community college, you can pursue any of those vocations crooned by Bob Seger 'cause Northwestern Michigan College partners with 8 universities (EMU, WMU, CMU, MSU, Ferris State, Grand Valley State, Spring Arbor University, and Davenport University) to offer bachelor, graduate, and doctoral degrees all while studying right in Traverse City at the NMC's University Center.

Northwestern Michigan College is located 2 miles east of Clinch Park, the end of this chapter's paddling trip. Commonly referred to as NMC, the school was founded in 1951 as the state of Michigan's first community college. NMC established another first when, in 2013, it became the first community college in Michigan to offer its own fully accredited bachelor's degree - a bachelor of science in maritime technology.

NMC established their Great Lakes Maritime Academy in 1969, teaching students navigation, piloting, steam and diesel engineering, and seamanship. The academy experience includes 276 days of commercial sea time. Today, this academy is 1 of only 7 in the entire USA, and the only one located on a body of freshwater. Here's another nice number: NMC's Great Lakes Maritime Academy can claim 100% employment for their graduates.

The NMC reach extends beyond the maritime students, teaching annually over 50,000 learners including non-credit classes to over 10,000 local residents.

The Dennos Museum Center opened in 1991 and is recognized as a premier cultural facility in northern Michigan. This NMC star features exhibitions & programs in the visual arts, sciences and performing arts, an interactive Discovery Gallery, a sculpture court (works of Michigan and international artists surround the museum), the Milliken Auditorium, and the Museum Store. The DMC owns one of the most historically complete collections of *Inuit art of the Canadian Arctic* in the USA. The Dennos Museum Center has been recognized by *ArtServe Michigan* with the Governor's Award for Arts and Culture.

The Joseph H. Rogers Observatory resides 6 miles south of the Northwestern Michigan College campus. Joseph Rogers was a former NMC Science & Math Instructor/Division Director who led the effort to build a permanent home for NMC's portable telescope.

Since its 1981 completion, over 100,000 have visited the observatory for monthly public viewings of the moon, Saturn, and Jupiter, and for rare celestial experiences like the Hale-Bopp comet in 1996 and in August 2003 when Mars made its closest approach to Earth in more than 50,000 years.

WNMC 90.7FM keeps the campus community humming. A recent listen heard a great run of Artie Shaw and Duke Ellington tunes during the "Jazz From the Tradition" show. A wide variety of musical tastes are met with station segments including "Folk Aire", "Blue Soul", "Canal Latino", and the wonderfully named "Cosmic Slop" featuring rock, alternative and electronic.

"In every way, the Northwestern Michigan College is a people's college. It was conceived in a regional desire for education and is being financed from the pockets of the poor and rich alike."

-Traverse City Record-Eagle, September 17, 1951, celebrating the opening of the college

The Tavern #1: Brady's Bar, 401 S. Union, Traverse City MI 231-946-8153 (SE cor. Union and 7th Street, one block from the Boardman dam portage)

One foot was in the door when saucy waitress Wendy said, "c'mon in, the food's better than the service". How can you not love this place? AND $1 draft Pabsts? Rub down the goose bumps.

Brady's is a very popular tavern with a great, old time, locals/not-yupified, pub feel to it and a sweet looking back bar. Mag notes that Brady's, "is a friendly place", the over-riding feeling once inside.

Decorating a pub wall are signed Red Wing jerseys by Nick Lindstrom and Martin Lapointe, with Lapointe's signed to our waitress, "Wendy, happy same birthday date". The jerseys serve as a reminder that the Wings hold their pre-season training in town each year, as does the framed photo of Gordie Howe, Ted Lindsey, and Alex Delvecchio smoking victory cigars after another Stanley Cup is clinched.

The fare is reasonably priced. We had the blue gill (Thursday special) and an amazingly juicy third-pound burger "done to perfection", with sides of home-made kettle chips, not-too-creamy cole slaw, and a pickle with a great garlic taste. The menu includes homemade pizza, nachos, chicken tenders, and a Friday night fish fry. Waitress Wendy aka Martin Lapointe's astrological soul-mate, sez Brady favorites are the broasters, blue gill, and BLTs. An excellent sign: a huge group of people crowd in here for lunch.

Brady's pizza wins first or second place annually in county-wide competition and, during our visit, just won their second-in-a-row award as Traverse City's "red-hot best neighborhood bar".

Waitress Wendy, full name Wendy Blodgett, has the ideal personality to be in this business, and shared some Brady's wisdom with us... *when the guys pull up in the back parking lot with ladders on the truck and dents in the truck doors, they're hard workers and have money to eat; the little old ladies come back time and again because the food's good; a common night-time sight in Brady's is the 26-year olds talking with the 80-year olds.*

The décor ranges from Ireland to Ireland and Ireland yet again, to golf, fishing and hunting. Both of the tavern pool tables were in use. 4 big screen TVs entertained several regulars sitting at the bar, inspiring their running commentary about the Tigers-White Sox televised afternoon game.

This building has staying power: Prior to current owners Pat Cole and the Cole Family (circa 1969), the previous owner was Bun Brady. Its existence goes all the way back to 1864 when this structure housed the old Union Hotel.

The Tavern #2: The Filling Station Microbrewery, 642 Railroad Pl, Traverse City MI 49686; (231) 946-8168; www.thefillingstationmicrobrewery.com.

"Just a few feet from the railroad tracks, you can get anything you want (well, at least beer, pizza, and salad) at the Filling Station Res-tau-rant"

One football field in distance to the north of the Boardman launch site at Hull Park sits the Filling Station Microbrewery. The gorgeous view of Boardman Lake draws the discerning diner outside when warm, while inside comforts during cold days. Though a limited menu, we loved the food. The many combinations of wood-fired, flat bread pizza plus 4 large salad choices, in addition to a kids' menu, satisfies even pan-pizza guys 'n gals.

Almost every townie we asked told us that the Filling Station is one of their favorites. The microbrewery features a rotating list of 10 craft beers. There is no Pabst or any other old-time, staid, what-your- grandfather-drank, beer in sight, but it was found that bottles of Wild Bill's Root Beer goes real nice with the Filling Station flat bread pizza and salad (there's also free refills on the fountain soft drinks).

The pizza was out within 5 minutes of ordering. Mm... one could get used to this wood-fired way of living. Olive oil, artichokes, mushrooms on one pizza, and marinara, tomatoes, sausage, thick bacon on the other pizza received "delicious!" reviews from all 4 diners, a happy way to end a paddle down the Boardman.

Chapter Sources: Norman R. Fred – Chairman of the Boardman River Clean Sweep (non-profit river cleanup organization), Wendy Blodgett, www.nmc.edu

Chippewa River / Central Michigan University

Degree of Paddling Difficulty: beginner (level 1 of 3)

Livery: Chippewa River Outfitters, 3763 S. Lincoln Road, Mount Pleasant MI 48858; (989) 772-5474; www.chipoutfitters.com. The livery offers hauling and car spotting services.

River Quote: "50... been there, done that, don't remember it" – Mister P

Chippewa River Soundtrack: Riders on the Storm – the Doors, In Your Neighborhood – Those Transatlantics, Roll on River – Okee Dokee Brothers, Waitin' For the Wind – Spooky Tooth, Hungarian Dance No. 5 – CMU Orchestra

Detroit Tigers radio station: listen to WQBX 104.9FM to follow the Tigers when paddling the Chippewa River near the CMU campus.

Directions to the launch site: to Deerfield Nature Park, take M20/Remus Road west from Mount Pleasant, entrance is on the south side of M20; park address is 2425 W. Remus Road (M20), Mount Pleasant MI 48858, phone (989) 772-2879 or 0911 ext. 340. Restrooms available.

Directions to the take-out: take Mount Pleasant Business Route 127 to Broomfield Road and take Broomfield Road west to Lincoln Road; take Lincoln Road north past the Chippewa River Outfitters livery – the dirt access to the river is on the southeast side of the Lincoln Road Bridge. No restrooms at take-out.

Background of the Chippewa River:

The headwaters of the 92-mile long Chippewa River form south of US10 and to the immediate west of M66 by the town of Barryton. From Barryton, the Chippewa flows east through Mount Pleasant and then into Midland where it ends at its confluence with the Tittabawassee River under *the Tridge*, a magnificent 3-legged wooden footbridge that spans the meeting of the two rivers.

The Chippewa River's gentle flow is occasionally broken by light rapids, bringing a nice change of pace to this beautiful river. A great wildlife experience (the most blue herons ever viewed on a river trip), paddling the Chippewa takes you through a shallow riverbed that is for the most part 1' to 3' deep. Anglers fish the river for bluegill, bullhead, steelhead, northern pike, walleye, smallmouth bass, largemouth bass and sunfish.

Educating folks of all ages about the caring for and enjoyment of the Chippewa River and its surrounding land is a mission of the Chippewa Nature Center. The CNC's Visitor Center and 15 miles of trails near the river are worth a visit. The Center is located near the eastern end of the Chippewa River's 92-mile meander, at 400 S. Badour in Midland MI 48640, (989) 631-0830, www.chippewanaturecenter.org.

Camping: The 591-acre Deerfield Nature Park adjoins the banks of the Chippewa. Upstream from the canoe/kayak access are 10 primitive campsites that may be canoed or kayaked to or reached by a 1 mile hike from the river. Deerfield Park features 4 covered pavilions, restrooms, picnic areas, horseshoe pits, artesian well, 10 walking trails, and an 18-hole disc golf course. The park is located at 2425 W. Remus Road (M20) in Mount Pleasant MI 48858; (989) 772-2879 or 0911 ext. 30 www.isabellacounty. org/parks-information/deerfield-nature-park.

Paddling the Chippewa River:

Put in at the bay at Deerfield Nature Park and paddle out into the river, following its flow to your left (east). During the July trip, the depth of this stretch of the Chippewa River varied from bottom-scraping to 3' (the depth was 4' – 5' deep in April) and the width from 30' to 60'.

- Total trip 7.5 miles, 2 hours and 23 minutes (check livery website for trips up to 4.5 hrs.)

.5 miles/10 minutes: paddle by two midstream islands within the first 10 minutes; at the 10 minute mark a stone & dirt beach lies on the right bank; 2 minutes downstream a "Camp Weidman Canoe Landing" sign welcomes paddlers on the right shore, beyond the sign cascades a nice 75' long class 1 rapids run.

.7 miles/15 minutes: paddle beneath the Vandecar Road Bridge; a long midstream island, passable both left and right, becomes visible downstream from the bridge.

2.2 miles/44 minutes: on the right shore watch for a home with a metal seawall and a multi-tiered landscape – it heralds a blue heron nesting area nearby: 6 blue herons have been flying above and ahead of us for 20 minutes!

2.8 miles/55 minutes: the now very shallow river runs through a long, boulder field – stay to the right; beyond the left shore are several beautiful homes.

3.2 miles/1 hour: at approximately the one hour mark and on the left, a home has a large deck that extends out over the river; their neighbors have a shoreline gazebo and an in-ground pool.

4 miles/1 hour and 17 minutes: canoe and kayak below the Meridian Road Bridge.

4.2 miles/1 hour and 22 minutes: an excellent place to take a break! On the left, the Meridian County Park access features a park bench and restrooms,

4.6 miles/1 hour and 30 minutes: a wide creek merges from the right, big enough to canoe or kayak if side exploration trips interest you.

4.8 miles/1 hour and 34 minutes: Johnson Creek merges right, 40' wide at its mouth and as wide as the Chippewa River itself.

5 miles/1 hour and 37 minutes: the holes in the 20' tall sandy hillside on the left serve as a bird sanctuary; 5 minutes downstream, a great sandy beach on the left makes another fine place to take a river break.

5.5 miles/1 hour and 46 minutes: the paddlers are delighted with sightings of sandhill cranes, river otters, and blue herons; the home on the right with its huge deck and built-in pool is the 2nd of 2 large homes.

5.8 miles/1 hour and 53 minutes: the fast-moving tributary merging from the left is the North Branch of the Chippewa River.

6 miles/1 hour and 55 minutes: reach the western edge of the Riverwood Golf Resort.

6.4 miles/2 hours: pass below the 1st of 3 golf course pedestrian bridges.

6.8 miles/2 hours and 10 minutes: as you approach the upstream end of a large island, note the painted yellow arrows pointing to the left – follow the arrows left.

7 miles/2 hours and 16 minutes: arrive at the downstream end of the island.

7.5 miles/2 hours and 23 minutes: you're in! Go beneath the Lincoln Road Bridge and immediately exit on the right. Chippewa River Outfitters is a 100 yard walk to your right (south) on the dirt path along Lincoln Road.

The Chippewa River Crack Research Team: Paul "Mister P" Pienta, JJ Johnson, Doc

The College: Central Michigan University

1200 S. Franklin Street, Mount Pleasant, MI 48859, phone 989-774-4000; www. cmich.edu.

On September 13, 1892, *Central Michigan Normal School and Business Institute* opened their doors, becoming the second "normal" (i.e. a school for training teachers) college in Michigan. Central Michigan Normal filled a need to train teachers for the quickly expanding rural school system in Michigan (urban school needs for teachers were being filled by graduates of Michigan State Normal College, the first normal school in the state and what would later become known as Eastern Michigan University).

In 1895, the Michigan State Board of Education assumed control of the school and shortened its name to Central Michigan Normal School. By the first decade of the 1900s, Central grads were teaching in schools well beyond Michigan's rural areas, making an impact in Canada, Puerto Rico and the Philippines.

The name changes continued... Central State Teachers College... Central Michigan College of Education... Central Michigan College (announcing the diversification in course studies beyond education)... until finally, on June 1, 1959, the institute name became what it is known as today, Central Michigan University.

CMU has gone well beyond its humble beginnings, offering degrees in a variety of the sciences, technology, law, communications, engineering, business, health professional – a total of over 200 programs at the undergraduate, master's, specialist and doctoral levels. A shortage of primary care physicians in Michigan is being addressed by CMU with the establishment of their College of Medicine in 2013.

CMU's College of Science and Technology offers a fantastic nature study experience to not only their own students, but to all interested: the 252 acres known as the *Neithercut Woodland*. The Woodland features miles of marked nature trails (including the "Freedom Trail," a 1/4 mile long, barrier-free hard surface, accessible to those with disabilities), a stream flowing through a forest of mixed hardwoods, and wetlands habitats ideal for both aquatic and terrestrial studies. Views in the Neithercut Woodland includes marshland, wildflowers, plants, and animals in a great variety of habitats. The Woodland is to the northwest of the main campus, off M115 northwest of the US10 and M115 intersection, at 4105 Cadillac Drive in Farwell MI 48622.

The CMU Biological Station on Beaver Island (the largest island in Lake Michigan) provides a base for research projects attracting scientists from around the world. The Great Lakes research conducted from the Biological Station includes water quality and invasive species. For the island community and its visitors, CMU offers hands-on learning through various field trips, scientific cruises and seminars about the ecosystems and natural habitats on Beaver Island.

U.S. News & World Report ranks Central Michigan's online undergraduate program as #1 in the USA for 2014. How 'bout those Chippewas! Other top rankings enjoyed by CMU include...

*   Top 5 Safest Universities in Michigan, according to stateuniversity.com.

*   U.S. News & World Report #3 Graduate education programs for teachers & administrators.

*   #6 Best Online M.B.A. program in America.

*   7th in nation for number of students (536) participating in Alternative Break volunteer trips.

*   World Leader in SAP certification.

*   100% job placement for physical therapy, speech-language pathology and audiology grads.

*   1st neuroscience undergraduate degree program in Michigan. The program was also selected as the 2013 Undergraduate Program of the Year by the Society for Neuroscience.

*   The only Michigan university with an undergraduate degree in meteorology.

*   Only Michigan university and one of two in the Midwest operating an island research station.

*   Most teacher alumni in Michigan.

*   #1 Michigan college TV station, 13 years in a row, voted #2 in the nation by the Broadcast Education Association.

*   and Jeff Daniels almost graduated from CMU!

Central Michigan University continues to uphold the values inscribed upon its seal in 1892: Sapientia, Virtus, Amicitia – wisdom, virtue, and friendship. *Fire Up Chips!*

The Tavern: Marty's Bar, 123 S. Main Street, Mount Pleasant MI 48858; (989) 772-9142

Upon entering Marty's, Mister P asked waitress Lacey, "Do you have Pepsi?"

Lacey: "No, Coke"

Mister P, "Pepsi?"

Lacey, "Pabst?"

Yes, Marty's has Pabst on tap, among other choices (for folks not as demanding), and holds the oldest liquor license in Mount Pleasant. Two ladies working at another nearby tavern, a bit more upscale than we like, both directed us to Marty's (although they said good things about "The Bird" bar, too). We were also directed to Marty's by old friend Poochie whose daughter Meagan, a CMU alum, recalled the tavern as a place worth a visit. Turns out Marty's is a popular spot for both CMU students and locals.

Marty's waitresses Tracey and Lacey (not making this up) took excellent care of us, including taking the time to dig up old newspaper clippings about the bar and the building's history. The food was a great value and tasty, too. Marty's $7.50 steak dinner (8 oz. New York strip with potato and salad) is a well-known exceptional value, the $5 Marty's Sub with ham, hard salami, cheese, lettuce and juicy tomatoes had zero need for condiments as it was excellent, the third-pound burger at $3.75 was described by Mister P, after a long mmmm, as "one bite and you know it's right". The drinks are priced for a college student's budget, about half of what you might pay at many other establishments. $1.50 for Pabst on tap – that's what I'm talkin' about.

Packed into the small Marty's footprint are several TVs, a pool table, a bar you want to belly up to, all with a real comfortable feel - a place at which you could spend the better part of an afternoon. For smokers in cold weather, Marty's keeps a small, heated room with seating right outside the back door.

This building was originally a 1920s social club known as "the Transport" in honor of the nearby Transport Truck manufacturing plant, a popular spot for the plant workers. Once Prohibition ended in 1933, the club began to serve alcohol and was renamed the "Transport Bar" by then- owner Sam Cascarelli. Sam would drive to the Stroh's Brewing Company in Detroit, loading his car with cases of Stroh's to sell to his bar's patrons. The first Post-Prohibition beer sold in town was sold at Cascarelli's. For many years, before and until sometime after World War II, the bar was stag-only, no women allowed. The bar was renamed "Cascarelli's" in 1949 when sons Andy and Joe took over. When they added a kitchen in 1960, the bar became the first establishment in Mount Pleasant to sell alcohol <u>and</u> food.

After other folks owned the place for 65 years, Marty Naumes, aka "the legend", bought the bar in December 1987. Marty is a personable sort & a member of the Mount Pleasant Bowler's Hall of Fame. Maggie paid him a high compliment, saying "he's holding up well for a guy who's owned a bar for that many years", and that was before we knew he'd previously owned a bar in Mecosta for 7 years. Marty told us a friend said he looks like he hasn't aged. Marty told him that drinking McMasters Whiskey for all these years was the reason. The friend replied, "oh, you mean you're pickled." Definitely put Marty's Bar on your Mount Pleasant "to do" list.

Chapter Sources: <u>www.cmu.edu</u>, Marty's Bar

Clinton River / Oakland University

Degree of Paddling Difficulty: skilled (level 3 of 3)

Livery: Clinton River Canoe & Kayak, 916 Highlander, Lake Orion, MI 48362, (248) 421-3445; www.clintonriverkayak.com. The livery offers hauling and car spotting services.

River Quote: "That river bend was tighter than a yoga teacher" - Doc

Clinton River Soundtrack: Ohoopee River Bottomland – Larry John Wilson, 3/5 of a Mile in 10 Seconds – Jefferson Airplane, Overture to the Sun – Terry Tucker, Detroit Breakdown – J. Geils Band, Filthy McNasty – Oakland University Jazz Band

Detroit Tigers radio station: listen to WXYT 1270AM or 97.1FM to follow the Tigers when paddling the Clinton near the Oakland University campus.

Directions to the launch site: I75 North to M59E to exit 41B, south on Squirrel Road, cross over Clinton River and then turn right on to Squirrel Court. Turn right into Riverside Park, address 3311 Squirrel Court, Auburn Hills MI 48236. Restrooms available.

Directions to the take-out: I75 North to M59E to exit 42, north on Adams to Avon Road. Turn right on Avon, crossing over Livernois to River Crest Banquet Hall in Rochester Hills on the left, access in back, address 900 W. Avon in Rochester Hills MI 48307. No restrooms at take-out.

Background of the Clinton River:

The headwaters of the 80-mile long Clinton wind down from northwest of Pontiac, flowing east through Auburn Hills, Rochester Hills, Rochester, Shelby Township, Utica, Sterling Heights, Clinton Township, Mt. Clemens, and Harrison Township until finally emptying into Lake St. Clair.

Occasionally you hear stories of paddlers who worked their way down the Clinton in the 60s, 70s, 80s, and 90s, and each story would always reference the heavy debris, many obstructions, and numerous portages encountered. Today's Clinton River journey has become a friendlier recreational experience due primarily to the efforts of Jerry and Renee Reis, who opened their livery, Clinton River Canoe & Kayak, in 2009. Taking on the task with Dale Goolsby and others, and armed with chain saws, ropes, and winches, CRCK have cleared long stretches of the river, making it a fun canoe and kayak adventure due to their good-stewardship clean-up efforts.

The CRCK livery offers a series of one and two-hour trips (combine these for a longer paddle) on the Clinton, as far upstream as the Squirrel Road/Auburn Hills launch in this chapter. The skill levels needed to paddle these trips ranges from "beginner-friendly" to "experienced paddlers only!" including the wild run between Livernois and 2nd Street, christen by Jerry as "the paddle of the brave". Whether beginner or brave, Jerry and Renee will help make your day an enjoyable one by matching the paddling skills of your group with the appropriate section of the river. The Clinton, because of so many impervious surfaces beyond its riverbanks, is strongly impacted by heavy rains and is one of Michigan's fastest flooding rivers (the Clinton and the Rouge rivers probably rate as the state's nos. 1A and 1B, in either order, for quickly rising and falling water levels). Call Clinton River Canoe & Kayak for the most up-to-date water levels at (248) 421-3445.

Within the Riverside Park to Livernois Road trip detailed in this chapter, the river drops 60' for an average of 8' per mile through a river full of tight turns and fallen trees to maneuver around (plus 4 portages in the paddle taken for this book), testing your paddling skills, engaging your reflexes, leaving you wide-eyed, laughing, focused, tired, and excited.

The Clinton River Watershed Council is another wonderful steward of the water. Their stated mission is to *protect, enhance, and celebrate the Clinton River, its watershed, and Lake St. Clair.* The CRWC's annual river clean-up takes place each September at 16 different locations along the Clinton. The Council coordinates efforts with community groups, businesses & organizations in its efforts to keep the Clinton River and its watershed clean. To see all that they do, go to www.crwc.org. The group's address is 1115 W. Avon Road, Rochester Hills MI 48309, phone (248) 601-0606.

Fishermen on the Clinton tell us they catch rainbow, steelhead, bass, walleye, pike, catfish, suckers, creek chubs and the occasional sturgeon.

Camping: Addison Oaks County Park, 1480 West Romeo Road in Leonard MI 48367; phone (248) 693-2432; www.destinationoakland.com. This 1,140 acre park, 30 minutes north of the trip outlined in this chapter, is the nearest to the Clinton. The park has several scenic lakes and ponds, individual & group sites with full hookups, cabins for rent, swimming, trails for hiking and biking, and picnic shelters. Take M59 west to Rochester Road then north to Romeo Road. Turn left on Romeo (32 Mile Road) and in two miles is the Addison Oaks County Park.

Paddling the Clinton:

This June trip was taken in what the livery considers "normal" river conditions. Clinton River Canoe & Kayak do not put people on the river if the USGS height gage is below 1.6' or above 2.2'... the gage was at 2 even for this trip.

- Total trip 7.8 miles, 2 hours and 5 minutes (check livery website for trips up to 10 hours)

The Clinton River starting access is in Riverside Park alongside the River Trail walk. The park includes restrooms, 2 pavilions, picnic tables, grills, kids' play area, folks fishing from the shore, a man-made waterfall, and a historical marker (the first industries in Auburn Hills were located here in 1821, home to a dam and sawmill). The river winds gorgeously through the park, enticing you to grab a paddle and head downstream.

.2 mile/4 minutes: paddle below the Squirrel Road Bridge and through steady light rapids.

1 mile/15 minutes: you are beneath M59. Due to the large amount of riverside development on today's stretch of the Clinton, there is a great deal of wildlife squeezed within a 30' band of the river. Little let up in the rapids make the Clinton an exciting adventure.

1.2 miles/18 minutes: paddle under the Hamlin Road Bridge. The river is swift, the GPS noting the average moving speed at 3.8 miles per hour. Once past Hamlin you encounter an island with passage available right or left.

1.4 miles/23 minutes: pass beneath the beautiful brick "bridge to nowhere", connecting thick woods on the north to thick woods on the south. Small trees have begun growing in the cracks of the bridge.

1.8 miles/31 minutes: paddle through the money as you see the first of many large homes on today's journey. The rapids take a rare break and sunshine dances on the water's surface, underscoring the beauty of the river commonly called the MCR (Mighty Clinton River).

2 miles/32 minutes: from here on out, there is an increase in the number of boulders lining the river floor. The speed of the river gives you little time to maneuver around each – if you're fortunate enough to see them in time.

2.2 miles/37 minutes: just when you did not believe that the riverside homes could be any larger, big foots dot the hill on the right bank as the river turns left.

2.5 miles/42 minutes: an exhilarating long run of rapids, wrapping itself around several bends, concludes. Excellent!

2.7 miles/48 minutes: at first, the river appears to run straight ahead, but what you see coming at you is the merging waters of Galloway Creek; at the merger, the Clinton makes an extremely tight bend to the right.

3.3 miles/55 minutes: before the Adams Road Bridge, on the left shore a fawn is spotted in the tall grass, then a deer that doesn't move although we're within 20' of it. A few feet after the bridge is a pedestrian bridge that is a part of the River Trail walkway.

4.9 miles/1 hour and 25 minutes: you're beneath Old Hamlin Road. Blue herons and kingfishers are above and around the paddlers. The water looks dangerous and exciting ahead... we paddle up to it... it *is* dangerous and exciting (looks CAN be deceiving, but aren't always), white water crashing on mid-stream rocks the size of Pabst Blue Ribbon half-barrels... we don't normally try to avoid something that looks like a PBR half-barrel, but today we make an exception.

5.2 miles/1 hour and 30 minutes: paddle below Crooks Road.

The rapids and the river speed are at their peak; you are flying through each turn, forced to make split-second decisions as you pick your way around boulders that are upon your boat with only a moment's notice.

7.4 miles/1 hour and 58 minutes: after passing the Eagle's Landing totem pole/canoe rack (nice work of art by the Eagle Scouts!) on the right, you paddle beneath the bridge at Livernois Road.

7.5 miles/2 hours: paddle below the final bridge of today's trip, Avon Road.

7.8 miles/2 hours and 5 minutes: you are in! along the shore of the River Crest Banquet Hall on your right.

Clinton River Crack Research Team: Steve Arnosky, Dale Goolsby, Carl "Doubles" Verba, Doc

The College: Oakland University

2200 N. Squirrel Road, Rochester, MI 48309-4401, (248) 370-2100; www.oakland.edu.

Established in 1957, Oakland University sprawls across 1,443 rolling acres of wooded hills and meadows, so you really should never schedule back-to-back classes.

OU's Meadow Brook Farms and Meadow Brook Hall were owned by Matilda Dodge Wilson, widow of auto pioneer John Dodge, and her 2nd husband, lumber broker Alfred Wilson. Completed in 1929 at a cost of $4 million, Meadow Brook is considered to be one of the finest examples of Tudor-revival architecture in America.

In the mid-50s, Oakland County civic leaders, considering the county position as Michigan's second most populated, and with substantial projected growth, began looking at the idea of Oakland County having its own college. Alfred and Matilda Wilson were asked if they would donate part of their 1,443 acre estate to the University of Michigan to house a school of higher learning, i.e. a UM-Oakland Campus. Matilda, however, had served on the State Board of Agriculture, the governing body of Michigan State University, and approached MSU President, John Hannah, with this idea. With an offer from Matilda Wilson of her Meadow Brook land plus $2M for construction of campus buildings, the MSU Pres said, paraphrasing now, "Heck yeah!".

In September 1959, *Michigan State University–Oakland*, popularly referred to as "MSU-O", held its first classes with 570 students and 3 buildings. In 1963, MSU-O became known as Oakland University, and in 1970 the state granted Oakland U. autonomy from Michigan State as it appointed its first board of trustees. The university experienced steady growth over the next quarter-century, but it wasn't until 1995 and Dr. Gary D. Russi becoming president that the real explosion came: since then, enrollment has grown 50 percent to today's 20,000 students.

Oakland University offers 130 undergraduate degrees and 135 graduate degrees through the College of Arts and Sciences, Business Administration, Education and Human Services, Engineering and Computer Science, Health Sciences and Nursing, and the most recent addition:

In 2007, OU and Beaumont Hospitals announced a partnership to create a new medical school, the *Oakland University William Beaumont School of Medicine*, one of the few new medical schools founded in the U.S. in the past 25 years. The new medical school will go a long way toward closing the gap in the state's shortage of primary care physicians, as well as having a major impact on the region's economy, creating potentially thousands of related jobs and millions in revenue (beyond the estimated $500 million OU already adds annually to the region's economy).

Go Golden Grizzlies!

The Tavern: Duffy's Bar, 3320 Auburn Rd, Auburn Hills MI 48326; (248) 852-2222

Duffy's has an old time feel that belies its opening in 2009. Our waitri Taylor said that while Duffy's is known for its burgers, the best item on the menu is their chicken tenders. Oh Lord, Taylor knows what she is talking about. These are amazing and, forgive the sacrilege, better than those at Chick-fil-A. We don't know what Duffy's top-secret batter is, but awesome is the word we're looking for. Wow.

The burgers, even warmed up a day later, were – to quote Maggie – delicious, thank you! The fries that come with are also good, but do not hold up quite as well warmed up the next day as the burgers do. The pizza was fine, also holding its own a day later but, like everything else at Duffy's, the grub starts and ends with those chicken tenders.

Located just around the block from the Clinton River launch at Riverside Park, Duffy's is a great place to kick back after a day on the river... basic, nothing fancy, and comfortable. When a Pabst was ordered from Taylor, the couple at the next table commented on the choice with such warmth in their voices that the sun shone through the window and filled up ole' Duffy's.

Chapter Sources: Jerry Reis, Dale Goolsby, www.oakland.edu, www.meadowbrookhall.org

Escanaba River / Northern Michigan University

Degree of Paddling Difficulty: intermediate (level 2 of 3)

Livery: Soaring Eagle Outfitters (Joe & Son's Service Center), 93 North Pine, Gwinn MI 49841; (906) 346-9142/346-5341; www.uppelletstoves.com/upanimals.html. The livery offers hauling and car spotting services.

River Quote: "Only in the woods can I find solitude without loneliness" – John Voelker

Escanaba River Soundtrack: Way Up North - Flat Broke Blues Band; Take Me To the River – Talking Heads, Buckless Yooper – Jeff Daniels, Sunnyside Up - the Go Rounds, Blackberry Blossom – Northern Michigan University Orchestra

Detroit Tiger radio station: listen to WDMJ 1320AM to follow the Tigers when paddling the Escanaba River near the NMU campus.

Directions to the launch site: from Marquette, take 553 South for 15 miles to Gwinn. Turn right where 553 ends at 35/Pine Street. Take 35/Pine Street into town and, once

across the river, the Soaring Eagle Outfitters/Joe & Son's Service Center is on the left. Restrooms available.

Directions to the take-out: from the livery, cross over river and turn right on to Johnson Lake Road. Take Johnson Lake Road for 2 minutes to Iron Pin Road and turn right – follow Iron Pin Road for 20 minutes to the take-out on the right. No restrooms at take-out.

Background of the Escanaba:

In Gwinn, the Escanaba's East Branch and the Middle Branch merge to form the headwaters of the Main Branch. From here, the Main Branch flows south for 52 miles until it empties into the waters of Lake Michigan near the town of Escanaba. The stretch of the Escanaba outlined in this chapter takes you through a forest of Cedars, Pines, Birch, Popple, Elms, and Maples. The Escanaba has a reputation as an excellent trout stream, an angler's delight for brook, brown, and rainbow trout.

Working to protect the Escanaba is the Escanaba River Watershed Project, one of the newer state watershed protection groups. The ERWP developed out of a partnership between the DNR, Trout Unlimited, and the Escanaba River Association. The group's efforts are directed by monitoring water-quality data, quantifying the river flow, collecting habitat data, area studies, and tagging fish to determine their travel patterns. ERWP activities protect and improve the resources in the whole watershed, improve fishing for the general public and build a foundation to explore other opportunities on streams in the Upper Peninsula.

Camping: Horseshoe Lake Campground is a 60-acre campground stretched across 1,250' of lake frontage on Horseshoe Lake in Gwinn. The grounds have sites for tents, trailers, campers, and RVs. Log cabins are also available to rent. Canoes, paddle boats, and larger boats may be rented to explore Horseshoe Lake. A general store, restrooms, hot showers, full hook-up facilities, fire wood, and a laundromat are part of the camping amenities. The HLC address is 840 Horseshoe Lake Road in Gwinn MI 49841, phone (906) 346-9937, www.horseshoelakecampground.com. **Phone 906-346-9937**

Paddling the Escanaba River:

During our July trip, the water levels were considered "below" normal. In contrast, a previous Escanaba River trip that took place in "normal" (and higher) water levels, allowed us to paddle this same stretch of the river 30 minutes faster.

- Total trip 6.8 miles, 2 hours and 20 minutes (check livery website for trips up to 10 hours)

You put in along the banks of the Escanaba's East Branch, down the steps behind the Soaring Eagle livery (a launching option is at the Peter Nordeen Community Park across the street). Here the river is 20' wide and 2' deep.

Within 5 minutes of putting the paddle in the water, you're beneath a pedestrian bridge and into a pleasant but not too challenging run of rapids.

.3 mile/8 minutes: the Middle Branch merges from your right – you are now officially paddling the very headwaters of the Main Branch of the Escanaba. Lake Michigan lies 52 river miles downstream. The combined volume of the East and the Middle Branches has widened the river from 20' to 80', while no change in the 2' depth is noticed. Blue herons fly ahead of our small flotilla.

1 mile/22 minutes: a long, dead creek merges from the left, 10' wide at its mouth, precedes an active creek flowing in from your right. The river has now deepened to 5'.

1.3 miles/27 minutes: large river rocks, some protruding 2' above the waterline, precede a wooden footbridge crossing the river. It is now shallow enough midstream that boats scrape the river floor, with deeper paddling channels far left and, to a lesser degree, far right.

This begins a run of strong class 1/borderline class 2 rapids, taking you around several bends over the next 15 minutes to the 2 mile mark, and ending near the fine looking brown house on the left.

2.7 miles/54 minutes: on the right is a tiny waterfall near two streamside homes.

2.9 miles/1 hour: splashing into the river on your right is a spring/waterfall, small but loud. The bottom-scrapping has temporarily ended as the river now runs 4' deep.

3.2 miles/1 hour and 3 minutes: the deer stand on the left heralds the start of shallow water once again featuring light, class 1, rapids.

The river is beautifully dotted with trees bowing down from both shores, some having fallen hard for the river's charm. Occasional midstream rock gardens allow you to exercise your steering skills as you maneuver your way downstream. The Escanaba's waters spray the rocks poking up above its surface. Sun glistens on the river's surface as blue herons delightfully glide ahead. Ah, nature's movie screen.

4 miles/1 hour and 18 minutes: hiding among the shade of the leaning trees to the right, a pretty little spring flows into the river.

4.5 miles/1 hour and 30 minutes: the red, white, and blue whirly-gig (so christened by the Soaring Eagle livery) aka windsock is flying above the left bank.

5 miles/1 hour and 40 minutes: on the left shore are 2 tents and a fire pit – this is a small (30' x 30') grassy turn-out, between Iron Pin Road and the Escanaba River, that may be used as a camp area by the public.

5.6 miles/1 hour and 50 minutes: to the left, a dock in disrepair fronts a home with a deck; this scene is a few feet upstream from a small spring gushing into the river.

5.9 miles/1 hour and 57 minutes: "DA-LITE" is the fine looking wooden A-frame just beyond the right bank.

6.1 miles/2 hours: "Camp Nutten-Better" is the tin-roofed camo shack on the left.

6.5 miles/2 hours and 10 minutes: at a severe diagonal on the right is a small alcove.

6.8 miles/2 hours and 20 minutes: you are in! once under the power lines, the Iron Pin take-out is on the left shore.

Escanaba River Crack Research Team: Yoshi Schlager, Carl Hayden, Seiko, Doc

The College: Northern Michigan University

1401 Presque Isle Ave, Marquette, MI 49855, phone 906-227-1000; www.nmu.edu.

1899... the first known use of the word "automobile" takes place AND in Marquette, Michigan *Northern State Normal School* is born. The town of Marquette, named in honor of Pere (French for "Father") Marquette, Jesuit Missionary and great explorer, namesake of the Pere Marquette River, but let us get back to the college...

As the "normal" name indicates, NSNS was founded to educate teachers. In fact, educating teachers was the only program offered at Northern State Normal School for many years. The one change that did take place in the first few decades at the Marquette institute was its name: in 1927 Northern State Teachers College, 1942 Northern Michigan College of Education, and in 1955 Northern Michigan College.

The 1957 opening of the Mackinac Bridge, finally linking vehicle traffic between the Lower and Upper Peninsulas, contributed to surging enrollment in the late-50s and into the early-60s. A new state constitution was adopted in 1963, and Northern Michigan College was designated a comprehensive university, expanding beyond the dedicated teacher's school and becoming Northern Michigan University.

Today on NMU's 360-acre campus, 147 undergraduate and graduate degree programs are offered by the College of Arts and Sciences, the College of Business, the College of Health Sciences and Professional Studies. Northern's most popular undergrad degrees are in nursing, criminal justice, art and design, and elementary education and biology. The public university is one of only 3 in the state to also serve a community college role, with programs ranging from one year diplomas through master's degrees. In 2014, NMU introduced its first doctoral program, the Doctor of Nursing Practice.

It's uniquely Northern Michigan University...,

- Only USA university that offers 5 national Accrediting Agency for Clinical Laboratory Sciences.

- One of three USA universities with both diagnostic molecular science *and* cytogenetics programs.

- One of only two Michigan universities to have an entrepreneurship major.

- One of the few USA universities to offer degrees in ski management and wildland firefighting.

- 90% or better placement rate for graduates in business, clinical sciences, engineering technology, music education, line and power technician, and theater.

- 90% professional school admittance for their pre-medical and pre-dental students.

- Has programs in 42 of the 50 fastest growing occupations as identified in the "Training for Michigan's Hot Jobs" report.

The university is recognized as one of the USA's most wired & most densely wireless campuses, one of the country's first to own and operate a WiMAX (4G) network. NMU's work has been so innovative that President Obama chose the Northern campus to announce his national wireless initiative in 2011.

Another uniquely-cool-NMU is their two highly acclaimed leadership programs: the Student Leader Fellowship Program (SLFP) and the Superior Edge. Introduced in the 1990s, the SLFP is a nationally-recognized two-year leadership experience for 50 selected students each year, with a goal to develop competent, ethical, and community-centered leaders. In the Superior Edge, almost one-third of all students participate in the program's four "edges": citizenship, diversity awareness, leadership and real-world application of classroom theory. Along with these two programs, a campus volunteer center conducts extensive outreach throughout the Upper Peninsula. For all of these efforts, NMU is a Carnegie Foundation nationally-recognized "community-engaged campus", and recipient of the "2013 Engaged Campus of the Year Award" from Michigan Campus Compact.

NMU's Glenn T. Seaborg Science Complex is named in honor of Nobel laureate chemist, and native of nearby Ishpeming, Glenn Seaborg. The state-of-the-art venue and its over two dozen laboratories is home to mathematics and computer sciences, geography, chemistry, physics, biology, nursing, clinical laboratory sciences, and communication disorders departments. The Northern Michigan campus also includes the Thomas Fine Arts and Art and Design buildings, a university theater, an award-winning library, a university center, two art galleries, and the Superior Dome. The Superior Dome, built in 1991, is the home of the NMU Wildcat Football Team and the world's largest wooden dome at 14 stories high, constructed of 781 Douglas Fir beams and 108 miles of fir decking. The Dome also houses an Olympic training site for elite-level Greco-Roman wrestlers and weightlifters.

Before the football team played in the Dome, they had a fascinating 1970s turnaround story... the 1974 team did not win a single game, going 0-10, so few saw what was coming in 1975. That '75 team, quarterbacked by a fella named Steve Mariucci, took the NCAA Division II National Championship and a 13-1 record. Mariucci still holds two individual NMU Wildcat records with 47 career touchdown passes and 7,523 career yards of total offense.

Another outstanding Northern Michigan University graduate and one of Michigan's greatest personalities is John Voelker. John was a Michigan Supreme Court Justice, writer (pen name Robert Traver, author of "Anatomy of a Murder"), fly fisherman (take a minute to read his beautiful "Testament of a Fisherman") and Ishpeming native. Voelker had a deep love of nature, outdoors, and everything Upper Peninsula. His concern for over-development of the U.P. forced him to politely decline an invitation to attend the 1957 opening ceremonies for the Mackinac Bridge since, he said, that would conflict with his duties as president of the "Bomb the Bridge" committee.

For Northern's glory, fight for the Green and Gold – Go Wildcats!

The Tavern #1: The Gwinn Inn, 170 W. Flint Street, Gwinn MI 49841; (906) 346-9619

The glory of the old Gwinn Inn has been restored – the Pizza Machine is back, baby! New owner Paul re-established The Gwinn Inn in 2013, old pizza recipe and all. Regular visitors to the ancient building that houses the tavern can rest in peace, again. Previous bar owners, the ones that once made the tavern pizza famous for miles around, sold the bar a few years back... to an owner that tried to cut corners (cut corners? on a pizza?) on the classic recipe. As you would expect, folks showed their disapproval of this cheesy approach by staying away in droves. When the corner-cutter (frozen crusts? in The Gwinn Inn?) sold his frequently empty pub, Paul was there to right the ship – he not only brought back the old recipe, but hired back the earlier owners and authors of the classic recipe to make his pies. The old clientele came back, Gwinn is once again a favorite pizza destination, and everybody lived happily ever after – the end.

You can see The Gwinn Inn from the livery – go out the livery front door, turn left to the next intersection, turn right, and that pizza goodness will be inside you in before you know it. If in doubt on the directions, just follow the sound of live rock bands on weekends, and the daily aroma flowing sweetly from the pizza machine.

The Tavern #2: Blackrocks Brewery, 424 N. 3rd Street (at Michigan St.), Marquette MI 49855; (906) 273-1333; www.blackrocksbrewery.com. As soon as you walk inside, ceramic mugs are visible hanging from the ceiling above, waiting for their owners to use them during their frequent visits to this fine establishment (bar sign: "think of your mug as a magic wand – it may only be used by its rightful owner"). Also as soon as you walk in the front door, you are in line to order your first or next beer. What's this? Why is there a photo of Willie O'Ree, the Jackie Robinson of the National Hockey League (first black player in the NHL), next to the taps? Turns out that Willie is being honored by Blackrocks: they name one of their dark beers after him – a dark beer often suggested to those who've never before had a dark beer. Mister O'Ree is still acting as a pioneer half-a-century later. Nice.

All the beers offered are noted in chalk on the wall. Mm... only craft beers here. Asked the Blackrocks fella which craft beer taste the most like Pabst Blue Ribbon beer, he replied, "that would be *Grand Rabbits* – but it taste a lot better". I said that I find that hard to believe and he laughed as a man who understood where I was coming from. And then... I drank the Grand Rabbits and... it is the first craft beer that I really, really like. No, it's not PBR, let's not get all crazy, but, it is real good beer. Blackrocks does not sell food, so don't plan on grub with your grog here. This wonderful neighborhood brewery has very limited indoor seating. Outdoors, the patio offers more room but with not quite enough tables and chairs for the strong crowd Blackrocks pulls in (and that was on a Wednesday afternoon!). Blackrocks mugs are created by Brian Dalman, a local artisan who makes each in a 3-chambered wood-fired kiln. Hopefully Brian will not share the fate of Fawn Liebowitz... 1962 kiln explosion... moment of silence, please. Maybe a Grand Rabbits or two in her honor, or perhaps several Fawn Liebowitz' toasts spread out over a number of visits. Guess that means I'm coming back. I love it when a plan comes together.

Chapter Sources: Aaron at Soaring Eagle Outfitters, www.nmu.edu

Flint River / University of Michigan-Flint

Degree of Paddling Difficulty: beginner (level 1 of 1); also, see "NOTE" under the heading of "Paddling the Flint River".

Livery: for Flint River groups of 10 kayaks or more, call Glenn at Ike's Mobile Kayak, (989) 750-5251, www.ikeskayaks.com. Ike's also services the Chippewa, the Kawkawlin, the Cedar, the Tittabawassee, and the Pine (near Alma) rivers. The livery offers hauling & car spotting services.

River Quote: "Thus the newest form of transportation was making its debut over American waters with one of the oldest of all forms conspicuously in readiness, in case of trouble" – David McCullough referring to the precaution taken by Wilbur Wright during his 1909 historic flight over the Hudson River & twice around the Statue of Liberty, a flight witnessed by one million people; *the precaution*: a canoe attached to the bottom of the Wright Brothers new invention.

Flint River Soundtrack: I'm Your Captain – Grand Funk Railroad, Buick City – Whitney Morgan and the 78s, Beaver Dam Blues – The Matchsellers, Cry Me a River – Mad Dogs & Englishmen, Hymn to a Blue Hour – U of M-Flint Wind Symphony

Detroit Tigers radio affiliate: listen to WTRX 1330AM to follow the Tigers when paddling the Flint River near the UM Flint campus.

Directions to the launch site: I-75 to Flint 69 East to 475 North to exit 11/Carpenter Road; take Carpenter east 1.5 miles to Bray Road (at signs for Huckleberry Railroad/ Crossroads Village) and turn left. The Bray's access will be immediately on your right. Restrooms available.

Directions to the take-out: I-75 to Flint 69 to 475 North to exit 8A/Longway Boulevard; take service drive to 2nd Longway Street (westbound) & turn left. Follow Longway as it bends L by Holiday Inn Express on L and Farmers Market on R, road bends R with post office on L. Turn left at the post office on to E. Boulevard Drive; park between the post office & the "Campus Drive Private" street sign. The pedestrian bridge 100' to the west of the parking lot takes you across the river to the take-out along James P. Cole Dr. The pedestrian bridge is 100 yards upstream from the Hamilton Dam. No restrooms at take-out.

Background of the Flint River:

The 75-mile long Flint River has its headwaters by the village of Columbiaville, northeast of the city of Flint. From Columbiaville, the river meanders in a southwesterly direction until Flint where its flow turns to the northwest. It follows the northwest line until it merges with the Shiawassee River in the Shiawassee National Wildlife Refuge near Saginaw. Riverside industry caused the river much harm over the years, but the water quality has improved dramatically since the 90s (despite the Flint River drinking water disaster), and much of the credit for its recovery can be credited to the driving force known as the Flint River Watershed Coalition.

The Flint River Watershed Coalition has been serving as a steward of the Flint River since 1997, conducting river clean-up activities, monitoring water quality, enhancing environmental awareness in the watershed, and coordinating recreational activity in and along the river. The FRWC coordinates their efforts with riverside residents and businesses, and the success of their endeavors is seen in the increase of the population of fish - local fishermen were catching pike & bluegills - and insects in the Flint River and its tributaries, as well as heightened recreational use of the river and along its banks. The Coalition regularly posts their activities on Facebook with additional FRWC information available at www.flintriver.org.

12 minutes from the end of the trip outlined in this chapter, the Flint River Walking Trail begins on the south side of the river between Fifth Street and, to the west, Beach Street. At Beach Street, the FRWT crosses over the river and continues SW on the north side of the river past the Faber Dam, the Kettering University campus and Mott Park. The trail ends at Ballenger Highway and the McLaren Regional Medical Center on Flint's west side.

Camping: Wolverine Campground is in Columbiaville, near the Flint's headwaters, on the north shore of the Holloway Reservoir. Both primitive sites and sites with electricity are offered, as are group rates and senior rates. Should you prefer a site on the lake, a 3-night stay is required. Wolverine Campground is located at 7698 N. Baxter Rd. in Columbiaville MI 48421, phone 800-648-7275 ext. 6; www.geneseecountyparks.org/ pages/WolverineCampground.

Paddling the Flint River:

- Total trip 5.2 miles, 2 hours and 10 minutes (for other river trips, download from FRWC http://flintriver.org/blog/wp-content/uploads/2012/03/FRWS-Brochureoutside.pdf).

- This trip was paddled during April high water levels; the river depth is sufficient to canoe or kayak during any month when the stream is ice-free.

- NOTE: this trip takes you to within 100' of the Hamilton Dam; because it is so close to the dam, **DO SO AT YOUR OWN RISK**; unless the river is unusually high, the current leading to the take out (and thus the dam) is very slow and easy to exit; **HOWEVER, if you have any concerns about paddling so close to the dam, you should exit at the Vietnam Veteran's Park access, 1 mile upstream from the dam** and described at the 4 mile mark below. Keep in mind that river levels may vary by factors including snow pack melt and heavy rains AND that high water levels increase river speed. If you choose to continue past the Vietnam Veteran's Park, it is suggested before you paddle to scout out the approach to the take-out area in front of the dam.

The Bray's access allows easy entry into the river, has plenty of parking, a porta john, and a detailed Genesee County Park's map displaying the path of the Flint River as it flows into downtown Flint. Depart from Bray's access, immediately to the right of the pedestrian bridge.

.6 mile/15 minutes: the river bends right with a beautiful home high upon a left bank hill; the start of a run of nice homes on the left. A blue heron emerges from the brush ahead.

44

1.1 miles/25 minutes: through a tunnel of fine masonry work, a stream flows into the Flint from the right.

1.3 miles/31 minutes: a large creek merges from the left; paddling down it provided turtle and muskrat viewing. Blue heron nests tower 50' above the right shore.

1.7 miles/41 minutes: twin wooden decks on the left with a park bench between them are just upstream from a right shore merging creek. At the end of the straightaway is a large water tower where the river bends left. 2 deer graze near the edge of the left bank.

2 miles/50 minutes: paddle beneath a railroad bridge. Downstream on the right are large, boarded up, brick buildings, part of the old water treatment plant.

2.3 miles/55 minutes: Kearsley Creek flows into the Flint River from the left. 100' up the creek are some fine class 2 rapids running over a rock ledge.

2.5 miles/1 hour: you're under the Dort Highway Bridge.

2.7 miles/1 hour and 7 minutes: from left, a creek winds its way through a concrete tunnel on its way to the river. A woodchuck runs along the left bank.

2.8 miles/1 hour and 11 minutes: a chain pulley-operated dam with 6 vertical gates stretches across the river. Our crack research team paddled through the open gates – should they ever be closed, you may portage around the gates on the right shore.

3.2 miles/1 hour and 20 minutes: after passing beneath a vehicular bridge, I-475 runs parallel to the river along the right.

3.6 miles/1 hour and 29 minutes: a huge electrical grid stands beyond the right bank.

4 miles/1 hour and 45 minutes: after passing below the Hamilton Road Bridge, the Vietnam Veterans Park extends along the right shore with a cement boat ramp access, 1 mile upstream from the trip's take out. *End your trip here if you do not want to take out near the Hamilton Dam, 25 minutes downstream.* Businesses along James P. Cole Boulevard are on the right.

4.5 miles/1 hour and 52 minutes: beyond the left shore you see the Holiday Inn Express and then the Farmers Market. A deck on the left bank connects the Farmers Market to the river. The UM Flint buildings are now visible in the distance.

4.8 miles/1 hour and 58 minutes: paddle below the Fifth Avenue Bridge. Your vehicles are ahead and on the left. The majority of the UM-Flint buildings are beyond the left shore, while the W. S. White is the large campus classroom building on the right.

5.2 miles/2 hours and 10 minutes: you are in! After passing under the pedestrian bridge and the W.S. White Building on the right, the Hamilton Dam appears approximately 100 yards ahead. As soon as you pass below the pedestrian bridge, paddle to the right shore grassy plain where a gentle slope, just upstream from a willow tree, runs along the riverbank providing good take out ground.

Flint River Crack Research Team: Glenn Isenhart, Steve Arnosky, Vicki Schroeder, Bill Dunphy, Chris Weaks, Carl Verba, Yoshi Schlager, Doc

The College: University of Michigan-Flint

303 E. Kearsley St, Flint, MI 48502, phone 810-762-3300; www.umflint.edu.

September 23, 1956, was a fine Michigan day: at Briggs Stadium, the Tigers pounded Cleveland pitching for 19 hits, helping Frank Lary win his 20th game, an 11 to 1 Detroit victory (Harvey Kuenn was 5 for 5 and Al Kaline was 3 for 3). 70 miles northwest of Michigan and Trumbull, Flint Senior College held its first classes with 167 students in attendance.

Years before, in 1944, Flint's Board of Education made a formal request to the University of Michigan, asking UM to consider opening a satellite campus in Flint. In '47, the G.I. Bill payed the college tab for many returning vets, driving the need for more higher education classrooms and teachers, prompting UM's Board of Regents to fund a study to explore this possibility.

Affiliated with the University of Michigan since its 1956 beginnings, Flint Senior College had its name changed first to Flint College and then, in 1971, the UM Board of Regents changed the institute's name to the University of Michigan-Flint.

Until the late 1970s, UM-Flint was located where Mott College is today. As the 70s were coming to a close, the university began the move to today's riverfront campus in downtown Flint, with its modern buildings and amenities needed for the expanding student population. 2006 marked the half-century anniversary of the school, and in 2008 UM-Flint opened their first dormitories.

Since UMF's 50-year anniversary, they have received more than their share of accolades...

- In 2010, UM-Flint received the *Carnegie Classification for Civic Engagement Award* recognizing "campuses that are improving teaching and learning, producing research that makes a difference in communities, and revitalizing their civic and academic missions."

- In 2012, UM-Flint was selected as the first recipient of the *Engaged Campus of the Year Award*, presented by the Michigan Campus Compact.

- In 2015, UM-Flint received a "Best in the Midwest" rating from U.S. News and World Report.

UMF offers over 100 undergraduate and 18 master's degree programs. The UM-Flint campus has a strong international flavor to it, with over 40 countries represented among the school's 8,600 students, drawn by a prestigious University of Michigan degree at an out-of-state tuition that is less than half of that at UM's Ann Arbor campus.

The Tavern: Soggy Bottom Bar, 613 M.L. King Avenue, Flint MI 48502; 810-239-8058

A couple hundred feet north of where the Flint River flows below Saginaw Street is the Soggy Bottom Bar, also known as the unofficial "office annex" of the Flint River Watershed Council. Maggie said "I knew you'd like this place"; "why?"; "it's your kind of place – divey"... said with the utmost love and respect.

Oh my... I see in the cooler behind the bar PBR, Strohs, Carling, and – from the land of sky blue waters – Hamms, along with another 60 bottled beers. Guinness is one of 9 beers on tap. And then there was the extremely tasty bottled root beer, Goose Island "WBC"... mm, good!

Live entertainment includes bluegrass, jazz, and comedy. When the music is going to be too loud for the regulars, it is moved to the side room, where you'll also find table top hockey, darts, foosball, and a pool table. The back room holds another pool table and a cool seating area.

The food is fantastic. Everything is cooked fresh the day of your visit, nothing frozen. We chose the crab cake sliders and the wonderful "Porker" burger. The "Porker" includes 6 ounces of burger, slow-roasted pulled pork, Carolina slaw, pickles, bourbon BBQ, and bacon – Good God Almighty, which way do we steer?! Maggie gives the Porker a previously unheard of "3 thumbs up!" as the burger with pulled pork is done to perfection. You don't even need the slaw, pickles, bourbon BBQ, and bacon on the Porker, as good as all the rest of that stuff is. Yes, the Porker could go commando.

Oh, THAT's good root beer! We strongly suggest after your meal and before you head out the Soggy Bottom's front door, that you order fries and a WBC "Chicago Style" root beer chaser to go for the road, and you'll be driving in style.

Andrew ran the bar during our visit, doing a darn fine job of makin' sure the drinks and food keeps coming at you, the kind of guy you'd like running the bar at your party. Steve has owned the Soggy Bottom since 2003. Lift your glasses to a toast, "May Steve desire to own the Soggy Bottom for several more decades!"

Chapter Sources: Rebecca Fedewa, <u>www.umflint.edu</u>

Grand River / Grand Valley State University

Degree of Paddling Difficulty: beginner friendly (level 1 of 3)

Livery: Lakeshore Kayak Rental, 14023 Green Street, Grand Haven MI 49417; (616) 566-1325; www.lakeshorekayakrental.com.

River Quote: "If it doesn't have a beer on it, it's not a real boat" – Captain Johnny Harcourt

Grand River Soundtrack: Rambles of Spring (live at Quinn & Tuite's) – Conklin Ceili Band, Wide River – Steve Miller Band, Dry County – B52s, High Hopes – Frank Sinatra, Beethoven Symphony No. 5 Movement 1 – GVSU Symphony Orchestra

Detroit Tigers radio station: listen to WOOD 1300AM to follow the Tigers when paddling the Grand River near the Grand Valley State University campus.

Directions to the launch site: I-196 to exit 69B/Baldwin Street, west to Cottonwood Drive & at a slight left Cottonwood becomes Fillmore; take Fillmore to 28th Street and turn north into Grand River Park, 9473 28th Street, Jenison MI 49428. The 162-acre park has 3 miles of hiking trails, grills, picnic tables, picnic building (may be reserved), a playground, and restrooms.

Directions to the take-out: I-96 to exit 16, south on 68th Street (Eastmanville Road), cross over the Grand River and turn right into the Eastmanville Landing. Restrooms available. The barrier-free launch deck has elevated aluminum bars and a transfer system to assist disabled paddlers.

Background of the Grand River:

Michigan's longest river is the 260-mile Grand River. From headwaters near the south central Michigan village of Liberty, its initial flow takes paddlers north through the towns of Jackson and Lansing. In Lansing, the Grand turns to the west/northwest, meandering through Portland, Ionia, Grand Rapids, until finally emptying into Lake Michigan in the gorgeous lakeshore community of Grand Haven. Along its 260 miles, the tributaries absorbed by the Grand include 6 that are over 50 miles long: the Red Cedar River in Lansing, the wonderfully-named Looking Glass River in Portland, the Maple River at Muir, the Flat River in Lowell, the Thornapple in Ada, and the Rogue River in Rockford. Local fishermen report catches of salmon, steelhead, brown trout, smallmouth bass, catfish, and walleye.

The trip outlined in this chapter takes place in the Lower Grand, about midway between Grand Rapids and Grand Haven. In the 1700s, French settlers traded with Native American villages along the Lower Grand by what is today Lowell, Ada, Grand Rapids, Grandville, and Spring Lake. In honor of the river's impressive width and length, the French christen it "Grande". While today the Grand is wide and flat, as late as the mid-1800s (until dams were constructed) there existed a wild rapids run through what is now downtown Grand Rapids: on a stretch of the river one mile long was an exhilarating 18' drop of the river's floor. The mental image of Native Americans flying through this mile of churning whitewater, flanked by fields of corn on each riverbank, while shouting for joy, is a beautiful one.

Caring for the Lower Grand is LGROW, acronym for the Lower Grand River Organization of Watersheds. LGROW has as its mission to "discover and restore all water resources and celebrate our shared water legacy throughout our entire Grand River Watershed community". Their efforts include educating riverside towns on ways to improve water quality, increasing environmental awareness in general, and heightening the effectiveness of all Lower Grand watershed groups. LGROW's website is www.lgrow.org.

Camping: the Conestoga Grand River Campground offers 81 riverfront sites. On the property is a camp store, full hook-up at all sites, horse shoe pits, basketball court, firewood, showers, pool, pavilion, restrooms, and rentals of canoes, kayaks, and pontoon boats. Their website is www.conestogacampground.com, address 9720 Oriole Drive in Coopersville MI 49404, phone (616) 837-6323.

Take I-96 to exit 16, go left/south on 68th Street to Leonard Street, right/west on Leonard to 96th Avenue and turn left/south. Take 96th to Oriole and turn right/west. The campground is on the left.

Paddling the Grand River:

- Total trip 8.6 miles, 3 hours (check the livery website for other Grand River trips)

The trip paddled for this book took place in July. Due to the width and depth of this section of the Grand River, canoeing and kayaking here has the feel of paddling in a lake, whether spring, summer, fall, or winter. At the Grand River Park launch, the river is approximately 250' across. Maple and Catalpa trees dot the shorelines, blocking visibility beyond the riverbanks. Note that when this river was paddled, an 11 mph headwind was present – on a windless day, the 3 hour paddling time would have been 15-20 minutes less.

.8 miles/21 minutes: a gap between the left (west) shore trees reveals a sloping green hill with a beautiful white home at its crest. The day of this trip, a large group of turkeys populated the hillside beneath an eagle's nest. Pseudo-doctor n' crack research team member Tom Holbrook says if you stay under the buzzing power lines stretched across the river, one becomes sterile within an undetermined period of time. Advice dispensed free, taken at your own risk.

1.1 miles/26 minutes: reach the upstream end of a midstream island. The downstream tip of the 1/10th mile long island presents a home on a left bluff with a fine looking deck.

1.9 miles/42 minutes: big creek merges on a severe diagonal from the right. Dead Ash trees, courtesy of the Emerald Ash Borers, are plentiful on the riverbanks.

2.4 miles/51 minutes: the building, the dock and launch site of the Grand Valley State Rowing Team takes up the left shore. Although much of the first half of this trip hugs the eastern boundary of the campus, the forest effectively blocks the view from the river of GVSU except for this peek of the rowing team. The dock location is at the upstream tip of a long island, an island that begins to the south of, and ends to the north of, the bridge in the distance...

2.6 miles/55 minutes: ... and you are now below that bridge in the distance, the divided highway of Lake Michigan Drive/M45.

2.7 miles/58 minutes: reach the end of the island that began south of the bridge. 100 yards downstream and on the right/east shore sits a private home that once was a restaurant and a tavern. A Detroit Tiger flag flies over the expansive deck of the now private residence!

3 miles/1 hour and 4 minutes: to the left, a creek 20' wide at its mouth merges with the Grand.

3.6 miles/1 hour and 20 minutes: at a diagonal right, a large creek with several homes on its banks flows into the river. A few moments later, paddle beneath telephone lines.

4.2 miles/1 hour and 33 minutes: on the right bank, a deer stand towers over a merging creek.

4.5 miles/1 hour and 38 minutes: reach the end of a 200 yard long island, left of midstream. You are near the beginning of a half-mile long river straightaway.

5 miles/1 hour and 50 minutes: with the town of Lamont and the traffic on Leonard Street in the distance to your right, several cows mingle at the river's edge, greeting passing paddlers.

5.9 miles/2 hours and 5 minutes: a large island dominates the middle of the Grand. On the right side of the island, two sandy beach areas provide rare good break spots along this stretch of the river. The island is 1/5th of a mile long.

6.5 miles/2 hours and 17 minutes: as the long straightaway makes a slight bend to the right, rising beyond the left bank a field of corn becomes visible between a gap in the trees. Tall Catalpa Trees with beans dangling from their stems and foliage the size of tobacco leaves dominate the landscape. 10 minutes downstream and to the left, beyond tall driftwood protruding above the river's surface, another field of corn rises on the slope.

7.1 miles/2 hours and 30 minutes: beyond the left bank sits barns, out buildings, and homes including a sweet lookin' white house that you'll miss if you don't look back one more time over your left shoulder.

7.6 miles/2 hours and 40 minutes: wide creek with homes on its banks merges right. A few feet down the Grand, deadwood piles up against the upstream end of a big island.

7.8 miles/2 hours and 47 minutes: reaching the end of the island, look to the right for the nice white home with two decks. After passing alongside a series of gorgeous homes on the right, paddle below the Eastmanville Road/68th Street Bridge...

8.6 miles/3 hours: you're in! at the Eastmanville Landing on the left.

Grand River Crack Research Team: Pam Carroll, Bruce Carroll, Gilda Weaks, Bernadette Kearns, Paula Brown, Karen Cripe, Jeff Cripe, Tyler VerMerris, Anya Miller, Cam VerMerris, Tom Holbrook, Doc

The College: Grand Valley State University

1 Campus Drive, Allendale, MI 49401-9403, phone (616) 331-5000; www.gvsu.edu.

Few Michigan colleges have grown in enrollment and reputation as much as Grand Valley State University, home of the Lakers, 4-time Division II national football champions. A college among the cornfields during its pioneer year in 1963, with an inaugural class of 226 students, GVSU has mushroomed from its original 876 acres along the Grand River to 1,400 acres and over 25,000 students enrolled today.

With the dramatic 1950s population surge in Grand Rapids and the surrounding counties, the Michigan state legislature saw a need for a 4-year college in the area. No one person did more to open the eyes of the legislature and the community to this need, and gain their support to fill it, than L. William Seidman, recognized as "the Father of Grand Valley State University". Armed with a convincing array of facts and figures, Seidman estimated that he made his pitch to a wide variety of organizations at over one hundred meetings in his effort to gain their backing for a 4-year institute of higher learning west of Lansing. Finally, on April 26, 1960, Michigan Governor G. Mennen Williams signed into law the bill authorizing the new college.

Grand Valley State University could not have asked for a more impressive and persuasive champion than L. William Seidman. The Grand Rapids native and businessman would go on to become an economic advisor to 3 U.S. Presidents (Ford, Reagan, and Bush I) and Chairman of the FDIC, among other national positions. During his days of working to make GVSU a reality, Seidman would begin each of his presentations by playing a recording of Frank Sinatra's big hit of the day, *"High Hopes"* ("Just what makes that little old ant think he'll move that rubber tree plant? He's got high hopes"), which must have been quite the attention getter as he prepared to tell his story. In 2013, GVSU opened the L. William Seidman College of Business Center, with a financial markets classroom, a stock ticker & computer terminals that allows students to track Wall Street, 42" interactive flat screens displaying financial data (plus one that can be viewed by those outside the Center), the Small Business and Technology Development Center, the Van Andel Global Trade Center, and the Center for Entrepreneurship.

Besides the Business College, GVSU is well known for its physical therapy, dance, education, film and video, and nursing therapy programs. The university ranks 10th nationally in the number of its students that study abroad. It has a 90% employment rate for its graduates. Grand Valley offers 86 undergraduate and 36 graduate degree programs from campuses in Grand Rapids and Holland, in addition to its main campus in Allendale, and from regional centers in Muskegon and Traverse City.

Each year since 1995, Grand Valley State University has been named one of America's 100 Best College Buys by Institutional Research and Evaluation, Inc. in Georgia. The designation is based on coupling the highest quality education at the lowest cost, and GVSU has made the list more times than any other Michigan college.

National Public Radio station WGVU FM 88.5/95.3 states its mission is to "provide educational, informative, and entertaining programs and events to the West Michigan community as a service of Grand Valley State University". The programming is excellent, led by the Morning Show's Shelley Irwin, an outstanding interviewer who has won five "Gracie Allen Awards" from *American Women in TV and Radio* for excellence as a program host. WGVU AM 1480/850 advertises itself as "Real Oldies" and, based on how Charlie Watts was knocking down the walls with his drumming on "Paint It Black" on a recent listen, perhaps the tag line should be changed to "Real <u>Awesome</u> Oldies".

The Grand Valley State Lakers are members of the GLIAC, Great Lakes Intercollegiate Athletic Conference, in NCAA Division II. Through 2015, the Lakers 4 national championships in football and 5 in Women's soccer are only two of the reasons that Grand Valley is a 7 time winner of the Director's Cup, awarded annually to the best NCAA Division II athletic program in the nation.

The Tavern: Main Street Pub, 11240 University Parkway (NW corner of 48th Street and M45/Lake Michigan Drive), Allendale MI 49401; (616) 895-1234; www.mainstpub.com.

It's difficult to find an old-timey pub in a county that was dry until the early-2000s, but the Main Street Pub will do just fine, thank you. When waiter Logan was asked if Pabst Blue Ribbon was available, he replied, "ah, a man of good taste". He told us that, among the beers offered daily on tap, all are served in 10 or 20 ounce mugs except one: poured into a 23 ounce schooner - because people demand more of the best - is Pabst Blue Ribbon Beer. Oh, Auntie Em, *there's no place like home, there's no place like home, there's no place like home...* In a group of 11 hungry paddlers, the food received unanimous high praise, whether for the appetizer skins or chicken fingers, the wraps, tuna melt, meatloaf, or the half-pound burgers (the Aloha Burger was described as "over the top" good, a meal surely created in honor of our dearly departed brother & crack researcher Marquis). Taking a walk on the wild side in a college town full of starving students, the Main Street Pub provides an all-day free food buffet every Friday.

In the main bar area, big screen TVs are everywhere numbering 16, along with a pool table, darts, video games, and juke box. For those seeking a quieter place to dine and drink, the side room offers a more sedate restaurant experience, with one big screen TV at each end of this section. Outdoor seating is available on two levels without much of a view but with plenty of fresh air.

"Here come the girls up the road, what they want to do they can't do, cause it's a... dry county" the B52s sing, but that's no longer the case along Lake Michigan Drive at the Main Street Pub.

Chapter Sources: Mary Holbrook, "The Grand" by Kit Lane, www.gvsu.edu

Grand River headwaters / Jackson College

Degree of Paddling Difficulty: beginner friendly (level 1 of 3)

Livery: although this section of the Grand is not serviced by a livery, GREAT (Grand River Environmental Action Team) schedules periodic headwaters trips, welcoming members and non-members to paddle with them. GREAT provides no charge canoes/kayaks to those in need if you let them know in advance. Check GREAT's website at www.great-mi.org.

River Quote: "I am haunted by waters" – Norman Maclean

Grand River Headwaters Soundtrack: Peace Like a River – Paul Simon, Low Rider – War, Old Man River – Sam Cooke, Rock Steady – Bad Company, Ventura Highway - America

Detroit Tigers radio affiliate: listen to WIBM 1450AM/101.9FM to follow the Tigers when paddling the Grand River headwaters near the Jackson College campus.

Directions to launch site: in Jackson MI, take I94 to exit 142/US127, and south on US127 for 13 miles to Liberty Road. Turn right/west on to Liberty Road and proceed 2 miles to Liberty MI and the Grand River headwaters at the Liberty Dam. Restrooms available.

Directions to take-out: in Jackson MI, take I94 to exit 142/US127, and south on US127 for 11 miles to Jefferson Road. The take-out is at the SW corner of US127 (aka Meridian Road) and Jefferson Road (Mobil Gas Station/convenience store is at the SE corner). No restrooms.

Background of the Grand River headwaters:

The Grand River is Michigan's longest. Its 260-mile journey begins by flowing north from the waters of Grand Lake, through marshland into the Liberty Mill Pond in the small town of Liberty MI. The Liberty Dam, the first & oldest dam on the Grand River, sits in the northeast corner of the Liberty Mill Pond. Bubbling over Liberty Dam are the river's headwaters, by the beginning of the 260 mile voyage. Largemouth bass, bluegill and northern pike are caught here.

In 1990, the first "Grand Expedition" took place, a once-every-ten-years group paddle of the entire length of the Grand River. The Expedition opens with a ceremony in the town of Liberty, paddling starting just east of Jackson at the Michigan Center Dam (the start of the river's north branch), and is completed as the Grand empties into Lake Michigan at Grand Haven. Along Liberty Road, just a few feet west of the Grand's headwaters, a commemorative stone honors the inaugural 1990 Expedition, placed by Michigan resident, state jewel, and river historian Jim Woodruff. Tradition demands that a cup of water from each of the Grand's tributaries douses the stone as part of past Grand Expedition festivities.

GREAT, the acronym for the Grand River Environmental Action Team, conducts an annual river clean-up of the Grand. Their efforts are a blessing to anyone who loves Michigan or its rivers. This paddling/environmental group also schedules 5-6 social outings on the state's rivers every year. GREAT's preparation for each of these canoeing/kayaking social outings become an unannounced river clean-up: in the week leading up to the headwaters trip described in this chapter, GREAT members spent 71 total hours along the paddling route, removing river debris and cutting/clearing fallen trees and branches that blocked the water. To check out GREAT's schedule and activities, go to their website www.great-mi.org.

Camping: the Waterloo State Recreation Area is the largest park in the Lower Peninsula. Located 20 minutes to the northeast of the Grand River's headwaters, Waterloo has 300 campsites, cabins, picnic areas, beaches, nature trails, equestrian trails, 11 fishing lakes, 47 hiking trails, and the Gerald Eddy Discovery Center. The park address is 16345 McClure Road, Chelsea MI 48118; phone (734) 475-8307.

Paddling the Grand River headwaters:

- Total trip 4 miles, 2 hours and 25 minutes (you can paddle the Grand for days - ten liveries service the river's 260 miles: go to www.canoeingmichiganrivers. com, click on "Michigan Lower Peninsula Liveries" and cursor down to "Grand River" to access each livery website)

Exploring the headwaters of Michigan's longest river is fascinating. Many only know the Grand as a 100' wide river crossed over on an I-96 bridge. To paddle the very beginning of the river's 260 miles, on a riverbed so narrow that, at times, you can simultaneously reach out and touch bushes leaning from both banks is a special treat... BUT, it is important to note that this is an extremely shallow section of the Grand: on the mid-May date that this trip took place, during a particularly dry spring, the river was so low that participants had to walk the boats downstream the first 15 minutes of the 2+ hours, with multiple stop-get-out-and-drag moments yet to come. It is recommended that, before committing to a Grand headwaters paddle, you scout the river's depth below Liberty Road (near the dam) and the next few feet (the most shallow section of this trip) OR inquire of GREAT through their website OR check the Jackson MI USGS gage at www.waterdate.usgs.gov/mi (this trip should gage above 10 cfps, cubic feet per second, before considering it). A March/April trip after winter snow pack melt or, at other times of the year after a heavy rain, IF the river is clear of debris (again, check with GREAT), may be your best bet.

.1 mile/3 minutes: gracefully cascading down a series of rocks on its way to the river, a pretty waterfall merges left, creating a lasting memory.

.5 mile/15 minutes: in higher (normal) spring-time water levels, the rocks on the river floor would create a sweet rapids run.

1 mile/40 minutes: paddle beneath the Culver Road Bridge.

2.1 miles/1 hour and 20 minutes: the boats glide through the first of many lily fields.

You experience a series of oxbows, one bend after another, down this entire 4 mile stretch of the Grand, with plentiful rocks on the river floor.

2.5 miles/1 hour and 30 minutes: from your left, a dead creeks flows into the river as you canoe and kayak through a water lily field. Yellow warblers fly alongside the paddlers. Another creek, this one a creek of lilies, merges from the left.

3 miles/1 hour and 55 minutes: you're paddling below the Gates Road Bridge.

4 miles/2 hours and 25 minutes: you are in! along the left bank and just before passing below US127. Visible on land are the Jefferson Road & Meridian (US127) Road intersection signs.

Grand Headwaters Crack Research Team: Mister P Pienta, Nancy Schlager, Yoshi Schlager, Eric Long and Doc. 40 additional boats were the guests of the GREAT team who invested 71 hours in the pre-paddle river cleanup (the GREAT cleanup crew included: Jim Seitz, Don Nelson, Kenny Price, Jack Ripstra, Tim Laning, Tim Weaver).

The College: Jackson College

2111 Emmons Road, Jackson MI 49201, phone 517-787-0800; www.jccmi.edu

After serving for half-a-century (1962-2013) as a Community College, it's a revelation to most folks to learn that Jackson Community College became a 4-year institution in 2013. The new Jackson College has come a long way since its modest beginnings: in 1928 founded as Jackson Junior College, the institute shared lab and library facilities with the town's high school.

Jackson College, student population 8,000, earned in 2013 4-year accreditation through developing curriculum for two new bachelor degree programs and expanding its international studies. Jackson degrees now provide career paths in the fields of Arts & Communications, Business, Management, Marketing & Technology, Engineering, Manufacturing & Industrial Technology, Health Sciences, Human Services, and Natural Resources & Agriscience.

The main campus is on Emmons Road, situated on scenic rural land 6 miles south of the city of Jackson. In addition to the Emmons Road property, the 500+ acres of Jackson College includes the L. J. Maher (North) Campus on 3000 Blake Road in Jackson, the Clyde E. LeTarte Center in Hillsdale, JC @ LISD TECH in Adrian, and the Jackson Flight Center at Reynolds Municipal Airport in Jackson. At the Flight Center, Jackson College offers individual pilot certification and an associate degree in Aviation Management.

Among the campus renovations taking place since 2011 are those at...

- the James McDivitt Hall, named in honor of the NASA astronaut and Jackson College student when it was known as Jackson Junior College (McDivitt received his degree in Aeronautical Engineering at the University of Michigan),

- the Victor Cuiss Fieldhouse, and

- the Rawal Center for Health Professions (formerly the Justin Whiting Hall).

The newly built William Atkinson Hall is a state-of-the-art Information Technology and Library building. Next door is a new Health Laboratory Center with classroom and lab space for nursing and allied health programs. Campus View 1 & 2 are new 96-bed campus housing complexes.

Jackson College student-athletes compete in a variety of Division II sports as the "Jackson College Jets", fielding baseball, softball, soccer, golf, basketball, golf & cross country teams.

The Tavern: Klavon's Pizza, 1361 E. McDevitt (M50), a few feet west of US127, Jackson MI 49203; (517) 782-8800; www.klavons.com

I know, I know, this is not the normal wonderfully old-time style tavern that I like to direct readers to. But the Chicago-style pizza at Klavon's is sooooooo good that I felt it was my duty to tell you about Klavon's. For me, Klavon's is better than any I've had in Chicago: better than Uno's, better than Gino's, Lou Malnati's, Giordano's, etc., and a convenient 5-minute drive (vs. 4 hours to Chicago) from the Grand River headwaters take-out: drive north on US127 from the Jefferson Road take-out, exit at M50, turn left at the exit, and as soon as you cross over US127 Klavon's is on your right.

Klavon's doesn't have Pabst – what?!? However, when I asked our waiter if they had Pabst, he replied "you mean Pabst Blue Ribbon Beer?" with such reverence that I couldn't help but be impressed (possibly the scent of the pizzas from nearby tables influenced my thinking) and renewed my faith in future generations. I settled for Mug Root Beer and its free refills, turning out to be a fine accompaniment to Klavon's pie.

Mister P informed me that his club sandwich with roast beef, turkey and bacon was outstanding (his verdict: "dy-no-mite!"), fine for those afflicted in such a way as to not demand Klavon's Chicago-style pizza as soon as they hit the door and are overwhelmed by the scent of superb pizza.

If you're at Klavon's you will not miss your favorite sporting events: in each room, at the bar, and (where you control the channel) in your booth are TV screens that allow you to follow the Tigers, Lions, Red Wings, Pistons, UM, MSU, EMU, WMU, CMU, etc. games.

Chapter Sources: Jim Seitz, Kenny Price, www.jccmi.edu

Huron River / Eastern Michigan University

Degree of Paddling Difficulty: beginner (level 1 of 3)

Livery: Heavner Canoe & Kayak Rental, 2775 Garden Road, Milford MI 48381; (248) 685-2379, www.heavnercanoe.com

River Quote: "We're proud to be part of EMU and don't consider the Huron representation as demeaning" – Les Cusher of the Huron-Wyandotte Tribe of Oklahoma

Huron River Soundtrack: Back To Ypsilanti – Lee Osler, How Long – Ace, There's So Much You Can Do in a Canoe – Brant Miller, Saturday in the Park – Chicago, Mozart Sinfonia Concertante - EMU Orchestra, My Little Buttercup – the Three Amigos

Detroit Tigers radio stations: listen to WTKA 1050AM to follow the Tigers when paddling the Huron near the Eastern Michigan University campus.

Directions to the launch site: Peninsular Park rests along the north bank of the Huron River at 1265 LeForge Rd. & Huron River Drive (across the river from Peninsular Place Apts.) in Ypsilanti. Launch near the old brick Peninsular Paper Co. downstream from

the dam. 2 sets of stairs lead down to the river – take the set nearest the brick building (at the parking area). No restrooms.

Directions to the take-out: just downstream from Waterworks Park is a dirt access on your left/ east side of the river, 100' before the Spring/Maus Street Bridge – do NOT park in this lot as it is patrolled and you may be towed; use the parking lot on the opposite/west side of the river, across Spring St. from the closed Ypsilanti Ford plant. Take Prospect south of Michigan Avenue to Maus/Spring Street and turn right (west) to access on right just before the bridge/park your vehicle in the parking lot on the right just after the bridge; OR take I-94 to the Huron Street exit, drive north to Spring Street and turn right/east, and drive to the parking lot on your left, just before the river, with the access on the left just past the river. No restrooms.

Background of the Huron River:

Ypsilanti's Riverside Park is the 2/3rds mark of the 129-mile long Huron River journey, 86 miles downstream from the headwaters that wind out of Big Lake in Springfield Township, and 43 miles upstream from the Lake Erie river mouth. From the Huron's beginnings northwest of Pontiac, its waters flow southwest through Milford to Dexter, where the Huron pivots to the southeast, following that line through Ann Arbor, Ypsilanti, Belleville, Flat Rock, to the town of Rockwood where the river empties into Lake Erie.

The Huron River trip outlined in this chapter flows slowly through a wide, shallow, rock and sand floor riverbed. Mink and muskrat populate the riverbanks. Smallmouth bass and carp swim by. Schultz Outfitters (a fishing, not a paddling, livery) on Cross Street in Ypsilanti's Depot Town runs guided fishing tours on the river.

No group does more to educate others about, or restore the water quality of, the Huron River than the Huron River Watershed Council. Since the organization was founded in 1965, the HRWC has effectively motivated government, business, and private citizens to become good stewards of the river. Primarily as a result of the Council's efforts, the Huron has earned a reputation as Michigan's cleanest urban river. To learn about their wide-ranging activities on behalf of the river and the entire watershed, go to www.hrwc.org.

No single person has done more to get people of all ages out on the Huron River than Alan Heavner, owner of Heavner Canoe & Kayak Livery. In fact, no one I've met in traveling the state and paddling 66 rivers, has done more to promote paddling across Michigan than Alan Heavner. Alan is a tireless and creative advocate of exploring Michigan, as exemplified through programs such as "No Child Left Inside" which has as its goal (from the Heavner website) *"to provide an experience so powerful that it creates a lasting impression and as a result they will continue to explore and enjoy the outdoors during their lifetime."* For info on all that is Heavner, go to www.heavnercanoe.com.

Camping: Ypsilanti's *Detroit Greenfield RV Park* offers 212 tent and RV sites and 5 one-room cabins. The park amenities include a lake for fishing and swimming, a playground, mini-golf, horseshoes, volleyball, game room, softball diamond, restrooms, laundry area, pavilion, and a general store. The park address is 6680 Bunton Road, Ypsilanti MI 48197, ph. (734) 482-7722; www.detroitgreenfield.com.

Paddling the Huron River:

- Total trip 2.1 miles, 45 minutes (check livery website for longer river trip options)

- A mink runs by as we launch along the northern boundary of the EMU campus and 200' downstream from the dam. Here the river is 80' wide and 6" deep. An August 1 paddle found the water levels slightly below "normal".

.3 mile/7 minutes: pass under the LeForge Bridge and through its light rapids; deer are seen running on two right bank dirt beaches.

.5 mile/11 minutes: the Huron deepens to 2'. Blue Herons and ducks fly by the paddlers in large numbers.

.6 mile/13 minutes: paddle beneath a railroad trestle and, 20' downstream, Forest Street. Nice rapids start below these two bridges and run 100' feet beyond. You are now passing along the western shore of Frog Island, past the trees on the left/east bank.

.9 mile/18 minutes: pass below the Cross Street Bridge (Depot Town and the Sidetrack Bar is to the left/east) and the 3-sided pedestrian "tridge" that connects Frog Island to the large park ahead and to the right/west, Riverside Park.

1 mile/20 minutes: reaching the pavilion and the deck at Riverside Park, you are exactly at the 2/3rds mark of the 129-mile long Huron River journey. It's a nice day for a White Wedding (MagDoc circa 1981). The small dirt beach on the far side of the pavilion presents a good take out spot.

1.3 miles/26 minutes: paddle beneath the Michigan Avenue/US12 Bridge. Outstanding rapids begin 200' upstream from, and end at, the bridge.

1.7 miles/34 minutes: you are under the rust-colored pedestrian bridge with Waterworks Park on the right bank. A fine dirt beach is on the left, 100' past the pedestrian bridge. A kingfisher walks along the right/west shore.

2.1 miles/45 minutes: you are in! at the dirt beach on the left shore, a few feet shy of the Spring Street Bridge.

Huron River Crack Research Team: Vid Marvin, Anya & Nathan Garcia, Gilda Weaks, Ashana Smith, Glenn & Lori Isenhart, Steve & Carol Arnosky, Paula Brown, Eric Long, Yoshi Schlager, Carl Verba, Ron & Ronnie Junior Swiecki, MagDoc.

The College: Eastern Michigan University

900 Oakwood Street, Ypsilanti, MI 48197, phone 734-487-1849; www.emich.edu

By 1960, the EMU student body's hunger for pizza opened up the eyes of two brothers to an opportunity to make some cash. In that year, James & Tom Monaghan purchased a pizzeria, Domi-nick's, located on Cross Street in Ypsilanti. In '61, Tom traded his Volkswagen Beetle to James for his half of the business, changed the pizzeria's name to Domino's Pizza, engineered a major expansion of Domino's stores over the next 2 decades, in 1983 (a particularly good year) opened pizzeria number 1,000 <u>AND</u> purchased the Detroit Tiger's just in time for their 1984 championship season - all because Eastern Michigan U students had a pizza craving in 1960.

EMU was founded in 1849 (thus the campus main phone number 734-487-1849) as Michigan State Normal School (*normal* is a college for training teachers). This institute of higher learning was the first teacher training school outside of the original 13 colonies and, when opened, only the 6th such school in the entire United States. Michigan State Normal School became Michigan State Normal College in 1899, the first college in the state to offer courses in industrial arts, business, home economics, music, occupational therapy, physical education, and special education. Acknowledging MSNC's continued diversification of the programs offered to students, the word "Normal" was dropped from the newly named Michigan State College in 1956. The final name change to Eastern Michigan University took place in 1959.

Deleting "Normal" from the college name did not reflect any slack in the success of creating classroom instructors throughout the years: today's EMU graduates more teachers than any other school in the country. In addition to the College of Education studies, Eastern offers programs through its Colleges of Business, Arts and Sciences, Health and Human Services, Technology, an Honors College and a Graduate School. Beyond the undergraduate or master's level courses are doctoral programs in Educational Leadership, Technology, and Psychology.

With 23,000 (including 5,000 graduate) students studying in 120 buildings spread out over 800 acres, Eastern Michigan University has been called "One of the Best in the Midwest" by *The Princeton Review* and recognized for its commitment to campus diversity by *U.S. News and World Report's: America's Best Colleges*.

The campus landscape is a beautiful meld of history and modern... from the Romanesque stone grandeur of Starkweather Hall (circa 1897) to the water fountains reflection off of the immense glass walls of the Student Center (2006) set alongside the lake oasis at 10-acre University Park... back in time to the art deco of the old student union at Charles McKenny Hall (1930) where today is housed the 700 pound "Bell from Old Main" aka the Meneely Bell, hung 1874-1915 in the tower of the Conservatory then in the Old Main until that building was demolished in 1948.

Although not technically on the Eastern campus, Ypsilanti's famous Water Tower is closely identified with EMU's student body. Visible looking north from Charles McKenny Hall is the grassy island where sits the stone statue of Greek General Demetrius Ypsilanti and the Water Tower. Built in 1889, the tower rises to a height of 147'. Originally constructed to supplement the town's water supply, it is listed on the U.S. National Register of Historic Places, and was the winner of a world-wide 2003 contest searching for the "World's Most Phallic Building".

When Michigan State Normal School became Michigan State Normal College in 1899, the nick-name of the "Normalites" was adopted. As the result of a 1929 contest sponsored by the Men's Union on campus, students and the MSNC athletic teams began to be referred to as "Hurons" in honor of the Native American Huron-Wendat (aka Wyandotte) tribe that had been based in southern Michigan. The Huron logo was shown as a dignified side view of a tribal member's head. The Wyandotte or Huron-Wendat tribe, now centered in Oklahoma, had consistently expressed their view (including directly to the EMU President) that they were proud to be a part of EMU and proud of how they were portrayed. In 1991, and with disregard for the feelings of the very Native American tribe that they were claiming to represent, the EMU administration decided to abandon the Huron logo for that of an eagle. The administration argument was that the use of a Native American as a logo or a mascot was politically incorrect and disrespectful. Were EMU leaders looking to solve a problem that didn't exist? If a Native American tribe finds pride in being associated with a university through a logo that honors that tribe, and if this pride has been expressed multiple times by tribal leaders to the university administration, is it not disrespectful to ignore their wishes and to treat them as if you know better than they?

The Tavern: Sidetrack Bar and Grill, 56 E. Cross Street, Ypsilanti MI 48198; (734) 483-1035; www.sidetrackbarandgrill.com.

The structure occupied by the Sidetrack was completed in 1850 and opened as a tavern, just one year after Eastern Michigan University was founded in 1849. Coincidence? I think not.

Love those bars that you can paddle right up to – and that list includes the Sidetrack. Well, technically there is a short walk from the Huron to the bar, but the stroll is short and well worth it: once you paddle below the Cross Street/Depot Town Bridge, and the very cool "tridge" just below the bridge, you're now in Riverside Park. Pull the boat over here for a Sidetrack break.

GQ Magazine has rated the Sidetrack burger as one of the "20 burgers you must eat before you die", while Oprah includes the Sidetrack burger on her "best of the best" list. Time Magazine has ranked Ypsilanti as the #2 among Burger Cities in the nation. In other words, in a burger town, this is the town's premier burger bar. On the dessert front, Maggie says that the bread pudding is the best that she has ever had, giving it an unheard off and perhaps mathematically improbable but amazingly satisfying "12 out of 10".

The Sidetrack has 34 beers on tap, but likes letting everyone know that if they're looking for Budweiser, they are out of luck, with the hash tag #sorrynotsorry. While laughing at their sense of humor, you can enjoy a bottle of Pabst Blue Ribbon beer, always a sure sign of quality.

The fantastic back bar, as well as most of the tavern's interior, is the original 1850 wood work. *Going to the 'Track for a burger 'n a beer* is an EMU tradition that is as old as the 1849-founded university – and that's not the only 'Track tradition…

In the early-1900s, off-track betting took place on the first floor, but riders on the train (railroad tracks run a few feet east of the bar) packed with men arriving from Detroit each morning were most interested in calling on Ma Bush's Girls of Ill Repute residing upstairs (to quote Glenn Quagmire, "giggity-giggity").

2 doors down from the Sidetrack, towards the river, is Café Ollie where you can get Sprecher's Root Beer (Milwaukee's finest non-alcoholic product) and Faygo Root Beer, Red and Orange pops – where's that Faygo Kid? Opposite the Sidetrack on Cross St. is a pub, Aubree's Pizzeria & Grill, that opened in 1972 as the Alibi, a little corner tavern and the frequent hangout of the ETT fraternity back in those early days (knocking a full point off their composite grade point; fat, drunk & stupid may be an underrated career path), and just another reason that Ypsi's best foot forward steps into Depot Town.

Chapter Sources: Sidetrack, Cory at Schultz Outfitters (Depot Town), HRWC, www.emich.edu, Huron-Wyandotte Tribe of Oklahoma

Huron River / University of Michigan

Degree of Paddling Difficulty: intermediate (level 2 of 3), exceeding a beginner rating due to the slightly challenging Argo Cascades.

Livery: Gallup Canoe Livery, 3000 Fuller Road, Ann Arbor MI 48105; (734) 794-6240; www.a2gov.org/canoe

River Quote: "It's rock solid and iffy" – Kanoe Kenny Umphrey

Huron River Soundtrack: Summer Breeze – Maitres, Can You Canoe? – the Okee Dokee Bros., Marine Boy – Haircut 100, School's Out – Alice Cooper, Hail to the Victors – UM Musical Theatre Class of 2015

Detroit Tigers radio station: listen to WTKA 1050AM to follow the Tigers when paddling the Huron near the University of Michigan campus.

Directions to the launch site: in Ann Arbor, M14 to exit 4/Barton Drive, Barton Drive east to Pontiac Trail. Turn right/south on Pontiac Trail, Pontiac Trail to Longshore

Drive and turn right/west. Longshore Drive to the launch at Argo Canoe Livery, 1055 Longshore Drive, Ann Arbor 48105, (734) 794-6241. Restrooms available.

Directions to the take-out: in Ann Arbor, US23 to exit 39/Geddes Road. Take Geddes Road west past Huron Parkway. On the west side of Huron Parkway, Geddes becomes Fuller Road and the Gallup Canoe Livery take-out will be on your left/south side of Fuller. Restrooms available.

- Pizza tip bonus: make sure you pick up a pizza or a "Faz" (folded over slice of pie), pre or post Huron paddling, from Hello Faz Pizza, 2259 W. Liberty Street near Stadium Avenue in Ann Arbor, (734) 741-7777, www.hellofazpizzaannarbormi. com. Nikki and the late and well-loved Faz Husain have run a pizzeria since the late-60s, in first Ypsilanti and then in neighboring Ann Arbor. Pizza so good it is almost as wonderful as Faz himself.

Background of the Huron River:

The Huron River meanders for 129 miles, from its headwaters northwest of Pontiac at Big Lake in Springfield Township, to the Lake Erie river mouth in the town of Rockwood. From the Huron's headwaters, its flows southwest through Milford to Dexter, where the Huron makes a pivot and starts a southeast journey through Ann Arbor, Ypsilanti, Belleville, Flat Rock, until it ends in the waters of Lake Erie at Rockwood. Huron River fishing in the Ann Arbor area is particularly good for smallmouth bass and rock bass.

The Border To Border trail, aka the BTB, is a walking, hiking, and biking trail running through Washtenaw County for 35 miles, much of it alongside the Huron's riverbanks. The trail is an off road connection of parks & educational facilities from Ann Arbor to Ypsilanti. The Friends of the Border To Border work to maintain and enhance, and increase awareness of, the trail. On their website are excellent BTB local maps along with a trail overview map. To access the maps and learn about various BTB events, go to www.bordertoborder.org.

The Huron River Watershed Council is an excellent steward of the Huron and its watershed. HRWC activities include monitoring water quality through a network of volunteers, educating private residents, businesses, and government agencies on how they can best interact with the river and watershed, minimizing both destruction of wetlands and conversion of natural habitat to streets and sidewalks, and much more. HRWC created an award-winning guidebook outlining drinking water protection plans that communities throughout Michigan are utilizing. Check out all that the Huron River Watershed Council does at their website, www.hrwc.org.

Camping: KC Campground in Milan is 20 minutes south of Ann Arbor. Whether you need a site for your tent or RV, primitive or electric, or you'd like to rent a cabin, KCC has you covered. The 20 acre campground includes a pond, horse shoe pits, a playground, a bath house, pavilion and a general store. There may be some guitar or banjo picking around a nearby campfire before the night's quiet hours. The KC

Campground is host to the annual Milan Bluegrass Festival, the first week each August. KCC is located at 14048 Sherman Road, Milan MI 48160; phone (734) 439-1076; www. kccampgroundmilan.com.

Paddling the Huron:

- Total trip 3.1 miles, 1 hr. & 22 minutes (see livery website for 2.5 hr. Barton-Gallup trip)

- A late-May trip takes you through this stretch at its "normal" water level, varying from bottom-scraping to 3' deep.

- ***Great Googly-Moogly! (in other words, this is FUN!)*** 2 minutes from launching at the Argo Canoe Livery, you are paddling through the 9 steps (each a mini-whitewater run) of the "Argo Cascades", a 10-minute ride through a man-made channel that allows you to bypass, and thus avoid portaging, the Argo Dam. The Argo Cascades "steps" may be described as a series of drop-pools. This is not suggested for beginner-level paddlers, only for those with the ability to steer a kayak through narrow gaps (the Gallup/Argo liveries only allow kayaks or tubes – not canoes - to traverse the Argo Cascades). The walking/hiking/biking Border-To-Border Trail meanders alongside the Argo Cascades.

.5 mile/15 minutes: you are beyond the Argo Cascades and now paddling in the shallow, rocky, flat water that will characterize the Huron until the Gallup take-out; to the left a major project is taking place to clean up PCBs left by Detroit Edison and then create, on the old Edison property, either a park or a mixed-use area.

1 mile/25 minutes: paddle beneath the Broadway Street/Plymouth Road Bridge (in the distance beyond the right bank, from upstream to downstream, is Casey's Tavern, the Amtrak Station, and the Gandy Dancer Restaurant). The western edge of Fuller Park is on Broadway Street. Soon the Kellogg Eye Center is on your left, behind Riverside Park along Canal Street.

1.3 mile/33 minutes: canoe & kayak under a pedestrian bridge and alongside Island Park on the left. The park features a Greek Revival shelter where weddings and other significant gatherings have been held, along with picnic tables, grills, 2 picnic shelters, a play area, and a path that winds around the island. The downstream end of Island Park has a boat ramp.

1.7 miles/42 minutes: paddle below Fuller Road. Visible ahead on the left are the buildings of the UM Health System and Mott's Children's Hospital.

1.8 miles/44 minutes: steps lead down to the Huron on your right from the Arboretum, better known as "the Arb", a site that served as a gorgeous picnic date spot during college days for decades. The Arb is a "naturalistic landscape" begun back in 1907 by O.C. Simonds, with peaks and valleys dotted with native and exotic trees and shrubs. 2 minutes downstream from the Arb's steps, you're below a pedestrian bridge and into the shallowest section along this part of the Huron, where we watched tubes get caught on the rocks. Stay far right after paddling beneath the bridge.

2.4 miles/1 hour: you're into a long straightaway, and the river is now 3' deep, the deepest encountered between the launch and the take-out.

2.8 miles/1 hour and 12 minutes: on your left, at the downstream end of Furstenburg Park, lies an island with pedestrian bridges on each end of the island, parallel to the Huron. Some folks have incorrectly turned left here and paddled under one/both of these bridges, believing that this is the way to the take-out. Instead, continue straight-ahead, where the Huron is widest, and past the next pedestrian bridge; only *then* turn left towards the take-out.

3.1 miles/1 hour and 22 minutes: you're in! at the Gallup Canoe Livery take-out on the left.

Huron River Research Team: the USMC Father & Son team of Jimmy & Spencer Vollmers, Olivia Vollmers, Vid Marvin, Carl "Doubles" Verba, Maggie and Doc

The College: University of Michigan – Ann Arbor

500 S. State Street, Ann Arbor MI 48109, phone 734-764-1817

2017 marks the bicentennial celebration for the University of Michigan. Established by the Northwest Territorial government as a "college for Detroit" in 1817, UM was built upon land once home to the Native American "People of the 3 Fires": the Ottawa, the Chippewa, and the Potawatomi tribes. In 1837, coinciding with the Michigan Territory achieving statehood, the college moved from Detroit to Ann Arbor. The small town nature of Ann Arbor, founded only 13 years prior to becoming home to UM, was underscored by the wheat fields and grazing cows covering much of the campus. Students in these early years paid no tuition, but were required to pay a $10 admissions fee and furnish "satisfactory testimonials of good moral character". Degrees could be earned from the Law, Medicine, and Literary Departments. UM was the first college in what was then considered to be the "western" United States to offer such degrees.

1866 was a landmark year for the institute of higher learning as Michigan, with 1,205 enrolled males, became the largest university in the country - it would be another 4 years before the fairer sex was admitted (although UM was one of the first large universities to allow women). From a "boys only" college to a culture of diversity has been a quite a transformation: today's student body pulls from all 50 states and over 100 foreign countries, contributing to 51,000 students at the 3 UM campuses. Almost one-half of the 51,000 come from the top 5% of their graduating high school class. These undergraduate and graduate students may choose studies from 17 colleges & schools and from 588 majors.

Student activism has had several prominent moments in UM campus life, and is never far from the surface (ex: Vietnam War sit-ins & teach-ins, Earth Day, the Michigan Mandate), and shows itself in public service with the prime example JFK's 1960 announcement on the formation of the Peace Corps on the steps of the Michigan Union.

The University of Michigan's reputation is remarkable, rated as one of the USA's top 3 public institutions of higher learning, considered to have the country's finest university library system, their computer access for teachers & students ranked among the nation's best, a health care complex that's one of the world's largest, the USA's #1 pre-law and #1 pre-med university with more undergrads accepted into medical schools than any other college's undergrads, and a faculty rated among the USA's top 5.

Research expenditures received and the ensuing medical, cultural, and social research activities undertaken are the country's largest with the bonus that UM students are among the first to learn the findings' applications. There are more UM grads in the fields of law, medicine, business, and engineering than from any other USA college.

That's all well and good, but why "Wolverines"? UM students and alumni began referring to themselves as Wolverines as early as 1861. One theory for this name was stated by the great Michigan football coach Fielding H. Yost. Coach Yost believed the origin of the nickname stemmed from the bartering of wolverine pelts at the Sault Ste. Marie trading post between Native Americans and French fur traders. The French called the pelts "Michigan wolverines" which led to the state nickname and eventually the adoption of the logo at the University of Michigan. A second theory has its basis in the 1835 border war between Michigan and Ohio for possession of Toledo and the final setting of the state line. During the dispute, Michiganders were called wolverines, either by Michigan folk who gave themselves the name to show their tenacity or by Ohioans who came up with the name in reference to, according to those people from down south, the wolverine's "gluttonous and aggressiveness". From then on, Michigan was labeled the "Wolverine state" and when the University of Michigan was founded, it took the nickname of the state it represented.

So which "Wolverine" theory seems more likely? The first theory is identified with a UM coach who won 6 national championships and had an all-time win/loss record of 180 & 37; the second theory is identified with a dispute that found the Michigan Territory trading Toledo to the state of Ohio for the Upper Peninsula (it's called karma); both events are extremely satisfying so we'll call it a draw.

The Tavern #1: Casey's Tavern, 304 Depot Street, Ann Arbor MI 48104; (734) 665-6775; www.caseys-tavern.com

Casey's Tavern is a Remy Hamilton kick (like the Wolverine's game winning field goal against Notre Dame in 1994) south of the Huron River, beyond the right bank at the one mile mark of the trip outlined in this chapter. This pub immediately grabs a paddlers' heart: when you step into the bar, look above the entry where a gorgeous wooden paddle, with much artistic detail, hangs.

Casey's has been filling bellies and wetting whistles (it is, after all, across the street from the Amtrak Station) since 1986. It is located in a building on the Historic Registry and the long-time home of the Washtenaw Lumber Company, so long-time that an old Casey's regular used to tell of driving his Model A to his lumber company job.

Relaxing in Casey's booths is fine, but to get the best view of the tavern, belly up to the bar. The back bar clearly pre-dates Casey's 1986 opening. Waitress Debbie, a hard-working, personable, wonderful source of everything Casey's, could tell us that the back bar was an Upper Peninsula creation from long ago. The back bar is more than just good for gazing at as it is home to 10 tappers (serving Labatt's, Guinness, and several craft beers), 20 bottled premium beers, 4 bottled light beers, and 4 longnecks including, saving the best for last, Pabst Blue Ribbon (by the "what'll you have? Pabst Blue Ribbon cold beer" sign).

Casey's menu included burgers (winning the pub multiple "Best Burger in Town" awards and an "8 out of 10" from the crack research team), appetizers, salads and soups (the mushroom soup earned a "10 out of 10"), hot dogs, sandwiches, and full meals. The weekly blackboard specials during our visit featured soups, fish, pasta, Mexican, and desserts.

Here a clubby atmosphere exists: the help has worked long enough to know everyone who came in. Except for a one year sabbatical, waitri Debbie has worked at Casey's since their 1986 opening, supporting the belief that this is a fine pub to work at. The bar walls are covered by 45 paintings, works of art by Michigan artists covering a variety of Ann Arbor scenes.

Casey's Tavern is open Monday-Saturday 11AM-11PM, closed Sundays. The back of their menu includes a 1776 quote by Samuel Johnson, "There is nothing which has yet been contrived by man by which so much happiness is produced as by a good tavern". Amen.

The Tavern #2: The Brown Jug, 1204 South University, Ann Arbor MI; (734) 761-3355; www.annarbor-brownjug.com

This is about as *University-of-Michigan-Wolverines* as the University of Michigan gets. Covering the bar's walls are UM still and action photos, team photos, magazine covers, menus from long ago, and signed photos from the many celebrities who've drank or eaten at The Brown Jug.

The bar's been opened since 1936 (although the menu mistakenly states 1938) and is named after the trophy that, since 1909, has been awarded to the winner of the Michigan-Minnesota football game, the Little Brown Jug. The story goes back to the 1903 6-6 tie between the two teams in a game played at the Minnesota Golden Gopher's home field. Upon returning home, the UM team realized they'd left their 5-gallon drinking jug behind and contacted Minnesota to ask that they return it. Minnesota replied that if UM wanted the jug, they could win it back (the next time the 2 teams played was in 1909) and annual game for the Little Brown Jug began.

The Brown Jug bar has an entire page of their menu devoted to shots of various spirits. Included is a listing of "stronger shots: warning!" with some interesting names... the Godfather (scotch and amaretto), Smoker's Cough (Jager and Mayonnaise - !?!), the Three Wise Men (Jim Beam, Jack Daniels, Johnnie Red), Rocket Fuel (Sambuca and 151), and the Jackson Five (Jack, Jim, Johnnie Red, Jose, and Jameson) – *as simple as do re mi, ABC, 1 2 3, de-sig-nate a driver for me.* You can wash any of the Jug's shots down with a 24 oz. can of Pabst Blue Ribbon Beer, or one of 11 beers on tap, or any from a wide variety of beer in bottles and cans.

The crack research team tasted a wide variety of menu items including "Jim Harbaugh's Meatball Sandwich" (judged "flavorful... very good"), the "D. Moss Hawaiian Burger" ("although the bar wasn't crowded, my burger was overcooked"), deep dish pizza ("it's no Loui's Pizza, but good"), hand-tossed pizza ("better than drive-in pizza"), J Long's Potato Skins ("they're good... I recommend the chicken over the pork"), and chicken wings and bread sticks (both judged to be "tasty").

Chapter Sources: Jimmy "Cool Papa" Vollmers, www.hrwc.org, www.umich.edu, www.bentley.umich.edu

Kalamazoo River / Albion College

Degree of Paddling Difficulty: intermediate (level 2 of 3) due to rapids in the last 10 minutes.

Livery: as this book went to print, there was no livery that services the Kalamazoo River near Albion College. The college does sign out canoes & kayaks to its students, faculty, and alumni – call (517) 629-1000. Also, the environmental/paddling group GREAT (acronym for the Grand River Environmental Action Team) schedules various trips down the Kalamazoo River near Albion every 1-2 years, providing canoes & kayaks on those trips – check www.great-mi.org.

River Quote: "I-Yi-Yi-Yi-Yi-Yiiiiii!" – Maggie's shout for joy paddling the Marengo Rapids

Kalamazoo River Soundtrack: Sea Journey – Stanley Clarke, Only So Much Oil in the Ground – Tower of Power, Floating – the Moody Blues, River Moldau – Smetana/ Philharmonia Slavonica, Fyte Onne (Albion Fight Song) - British Eighth Marching Band

Detroit Tigers radio stations: listen to WIBM 1450AM or 101.9FM to follow the Tigers when paddling the Kalamazoo near the Albion campus.

Directions to the launch site: I-94 west of Jackson to Albion exit 121/Business Route 94-M99, BR94-M99 south, cross over the river and continue to Erie Street. Turn left/east on Erie Street and drive to the Rieger Park entrance (just before the river) and turn right/south into the park. The access is ahead and on the left. Restrooms available.

Directions to the take-out: I-94 to Albion exit 115/22 ½ Mile Road, south on 22 ½ Mile Road to D Drive N and turn left/east. Take D Drive N to 23 Mile Road and turn right/south. Take 23 Mile Road to B Drive N and turn right/west. On B Drive N, cross over the river – the access will be on the right/north bank. No restrooms.

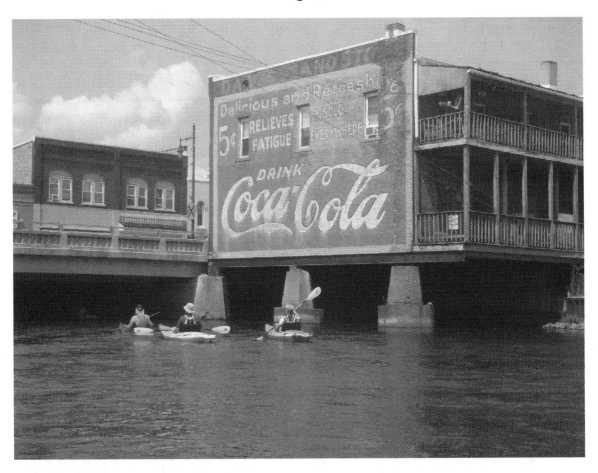

Background of the Kalamazoo River:

The 130-mile long Kalamazoo journey begins in Albion, where the North and South branches merge to form the river's headwaters. From Albion, the Kalamazoo meanders west/northwest through Marshall, Battle Creek, and Kalamazoo before flowing into Lake Michigan at Saugatuck. Pike, smallmouth and largemouth bass are plentiful in the river around Albion.

In 2010, not far downstream from the trip outlined in this chapter, the largest inland oil spill in United States history took place: the Enbridge Oil Spill. Just west of the town of Marshall, almost 1 million gallons of oil spewed from an Enbridge pipeline break in little Talmadge Creek. Since Talmadge Creek flows into the Kalamazoo River, so did the oil. The spill eventually spread down the Kalamazoo River for 40 miles, to Morrow Lake by the town of Kalamazoo, 80 miles short of Lake Michigan. Dredging operations to clean up the spill were conducted by Enbridge until 2014 when they declared the river clean-up complete. Regarding the spill, Christine Kosmowski, Calhoun County Water Resources Commissioner, said that from Marshall past Battle Creek, the smells from the spill were overwhelming for the first several weeks... to see the vegetation oiled and all of the wildlife effected was a horrendous thing. She added that, although the Enbridge dredging removed 350,000 cubic yards of river bottom, even that will not take out all of the submerged oiled soil. Newspaper reports suggest that, pending future technological advances, as much of 100,000 gallons of the 1M spilled may never be removed from the Kalamazoo River.

The annual summertime "Albion Flotilla" also known as the "Kanoe the Kazoo/Homer-Albion", promotes recreational use and increased environmental awareness of the Kalamazoo River in the Albion area. Sponsored by Albion College, the Rotary Club of Albion, the Albion Riverfront Development & Environmental Committee, and the Calhoun County Convention & Visitors Bureau, the Albion Flotilla is an 8 mile paddle, taking canoers and kayakers from Homer to Albion. Launching on the south branch of the river at the Grist Mill Park in Homer, this 3 hour journey ends just short of the merger of the south and north branches (together forming the main branch of the river) in Albion at the American Legion Hall. The "Kanoe the Kazoo/Homer-Albion" event provides water and protein bars for the trip, good eatin' at the Legion Hall, and bus transportation back to the vehicles in Homer. For more info or to register, call the Greater Albion Chamber of Commerce (517) 629-5533.

Camping: Getting good reviews and just a few minutes north of town is Rockey's Campground. Rockey's is on Bass Lake, part of a chain of 5 lakes, with a sandy beach for fishing & swimming. Set-up your tent, park the RV, or rent a cabin. Their amenities include a camp store, picnic tables, game room, laundry, hot showers, flush toilets, and a large pavilion. Rockey's is located at 19880 27 1/2 Mile Rd, Albion, MI 49224, ph. 517-857-2200; www.rockeyscampground.com.

Paddling the Kalamazoo River:

- Total trip 6.9 miles, 2 hours and 6 minutes (check www.great-mi.org for K-river options)

Put in at the public access at Rieger Park in downtown Albion on the Kazoo headwaters, on the South Branch of the river. The August paddle was at "normal" water levels. At launch, the river is very shallow, from bottom-scraping to 6" deep, and 40' wide. You immediately are paddling through a rock garden. The structure across from Rieger Park and built over the river is Emmons Horse & Carriage Barn, circa 1908. The river depth varies from bottom skimming to 4' and the width from 30' to 70'.

.2 mile/5 minutes: North Branch of Kalamazoo River merges from the right into the South Branch, forming the headwaters of the Main Branch.

Within the first 10 min of the trip in downtown Albion paddle beneath a series of bridges and a few old store buildings on Superior Street. Quite a few historic buildings dot the riverside.

.6 mile/10 minutes: paddle beneath Eaton Street Bridge. Just past the bridge, the Washington St. Park lies on the left. Here, the river is 2' deep and 30' wide.

.9 mile/18 minutes: riffles take you below the last downtown bridge at Albion Street. An old concrete structure with small columns (balusters) decorates the top half of the bridge.

1 mile/20 minutes: a pedestrian bridge, part of the Albion River Trail, crosses the Kalamazoo. The river has widened to 60'. Beyond the brush & trees on the left begins McClure Park.

Long straightaways now prevail, many requiring steering around debris fields of leaning trees, branches, and deadwood. The current speed is moderate at 3 mph. Reeds fill the river floor.

1.3 miles/25 minutes: paddle beneath power lines.

1.4 miles/29 minutes: left of midstream the upstream end of an island becomes visible, while beyond the right shore the Albion Wastewater Treatment Plant works.

1.8 miles/35 minutes: right of midstream lies a grassy island.

2.1 miles/41 minutes: big midstream island slightly right of midstream is the first of several in succession; pass on the left – very clogged on the right. The Continental Carbonic Products plant parks in the distance beyond the right bank.

2.8 miles/52 minutes: reach largest island you'll see today, may pass left or right.

3 miles/56 minutes: start to see large rocks on the river floor, occasionally poking their heads up above the water line, and along the river banks.

3.3 miles/1 hour: pass by homes, the first seen in 2 miles, beyond both shorelines.

3.5 miles/1 hour and 5 minutes: after paddling for 3 minutes alongside 25 & ½ Road on the left bank, paddle below the B Drive North Bridge.

3.8 miles/1 hour and 10 minutes: creek merges from right, 12' wide at its mouth.

4.1 miles/1 hour and 15 minutes: tiny "milkweed island" sits midstream; Railroad tracks run along right bank.

4.5 miles/1 hour and 22 minutes: class 1-2 rapids enliven the paddling at the left bend.

4.8 miles/1 hour and 30 minutes: shade extends across the Kalamazoo as you paddle through light rapids and under the power lines at the right river bend.

5.5 miles/1 hour and 40 minutes: short midstream island, 10' wide and 30' long, passable R or L.

Wear bright orange if you're canoeing or kayaking here in the fall – we're starting to paddle by a few hunting blinds.

5.9 miles/1 hour and 47 minutes: begin to paddle along several homes on the right shore.

6.2 miles/1 hour and 53 minutes: fine class one rapids take you below the 23 Mile Road/Broad Street Bridge.

6.3 miles/1 hour and 55 minutes: the river bends to the left and takes a big drop as you fly through the very challenging class 2 Marengo Rapids. Paddle through the rapids center and be aware of big rocks just below the surface as the rapids wind down. Islands just downstream offer beaches that make good break spots.

2 minutes past the rapids, two very large homes populate the left bank, the second one a beautiful wooden home.

6.6 miles/2 hours: the island left of midstream is passable on the right.

6.9 miles/2 hours and 6 minutes: you're in! at the upstream base of the B Drive North Bridge, take out at the dirt path on the right.

Kalamazoo Crack Research Team: the Grand River Environmental Action Team (GREAT) and MagDoc.

The College: Albion College

611 E. Porter St., Albion, Michigan 49224, phone 517-629-1000; www.albion.edu.

It's December 1994 in Salem, Virginia, and the Division III championship football game, aka the Amos Alonzo Stagg Bowl, has the Albion College Britons as huge underdogs to Washington & Jefferson, perennial D3 playoff participants and the overwhelming pre-season favorite to win it all. With the entire state of Michigan cheering them on, the Albion Britons reel off 31 unanswered points on their way to a no-doubt-about-it 38 to 15 championship victory.

Situated along the banks of the Kalamazoo River, Albion College, a private, liberal arts college, had its beginnings not in the town of Albion, but rather a few miles to the southeast. In 1835, two years before Michigan achieved statehood, the Michigan Territorial Legislature awarded a charter to Methodist settlers to create a seminary in Spring Arbor Township, south of Jackson. Before any classes could be held there, trustees applied to have the seminary transferred to Albion, and the legislature approved this in 1838.

In 1840, the cornerstone was laid for the first Albion building. By 1843, the institute opened for its first students under the name of the Wesleyan Seminary, with a mission to educate the children of area settlers and of Native Americans. By 1850, this early version of Albion College became one of the first co-ed schools in the Midwest when a sister school, the Albion Female Collegiate Institute, opened its doors. In 1857, the Wesleyan Seminary and the Albion Female Collegiate Institute merged into one campus, in 1861 renamed as Albion College, authorized by the state legislature to confer 4-year degrees to its students. An example of how intertwined the Methodists adherents were with Albion College: the world famous song, "The Old Rugged Cross", was written here in 1912 by Methodist Reverend George Bennard.

The center of today's 225-acre Albion College has not moved from where that first cornerstone was laid in 1840, in the area known as "the Quad", although the 2 buildings of 1861 have grown now to 30 to meet the needs of its 1500 students. Walking through the campus, you are struck by the beauty of its many century-old buildings and the landscape surrounding them. Included among those structures is the Kresge Gymnasium, opened in 1925 (with multiple renovations since) and the state of Michigan's oldest active intercollegiate athletic facility, and the beautiful 1845 gray stone of St. John's Church. Even newer buildings incorporate the school's early days including the 2002 restored Ferguson Administrative Building - located within the Quad, the Ferguson was designed with an arched brick entrance, a two-story copper clad cupola perched on its top, and 100 year-old marble mosaics from the old administration building.

Albion College offers a Bachelor of Arts degree and a Bachelor of Fine Arts degree, as well as 30 academic majors to earn those degrees. In addition, the college studies include pre-professional programs in pre-law, pre-med, pre-engineering, and pre-social work. Within Albion's "Programs of Distinction" is the *Gerald R. Ford Institute for Leadership in Public Policy and Service* with internships that place students in all levels of government, nonprofit organizations, the media, and the legal system.

Albion College achievements have been recognized by the national media in a number of ways:

- U.S. News & World Report's "America's Best Colleges" lists Albion as one of 40 "Great Colleges at Great Prices" across the United States.

- U.S. News & World Report ranks Albion among the Top 100 National Liberal Arts Colleges.

- The Princeton Review recognizes Albion College on their Best 380 Colleges list.

- Forbes America's Top Colleges list includes Albion.

- Washington Monthly's College Guide's Top 100 Midwest "Best Bang for the Buck", which rates schools based on their contribution to the public good, includes Albion.

- Albion College's campus sustainability efforts earned them a place in the Princeton Review's Guide to 353 Green Colleges, and notice as a "Cool School" by Sierra, the official magazine of the Sierra Club.

- Albion's teacher education program has been recognized as a Model of Excellence by the Association of Independent Liberal Arts Colleges for Teacher Education.

- In utilizing technology to develop their students, Albion College ranks among the best. They have been named multiple times to *Yahoo! Internet Life* magazine's "Top 10 Wired Colleges in America and folks from all over the world attended when Albion College hosted one of the nation's first "Internet Open Houses".

- The love of the Albion College experience comes back to the institute in a very tangible way: they are ranked among the top 20 of all colleges and universities in the percentage of alumni who donate to their alma mater.

The Tavern: Cascarelli's of Albion, 116 S. Superior Street, Albion MI 49224; (517) 629-3675; www.cascarellisalbion.com.

A true classic, old timey, tavern, Cascarelli's is a real comfortable pub to relax in after your day on the Kalamazoo River's headwaters. While walking across the Albion College campus, two people were stopped and asked for a suggestion on where to grab a bite in town. Yes, the sample was small, but the replies were strongly stated, "You want to go to Cascarelli's!"

So glad their advice was followed. The burgers and the pizza tasted great, and a campus guide said that the club sandwiches were the best item on the menu (sounds like a future meal). The clubs are one of 16 sandwiches on the menu, along with calzones, appetizers, salads, as well as the burgers & pizzas ordered by our crack research team.

The beers on tap include Pabst Blue Ribbon, always a sure sign of quality. On top of the back bar it's like *Toy Story* for adults with statues from the golden age of brew including the Pfeiffer Beer flute boy, the Drewrys Beer Canadian Mountie, a Blatz waiter with his head sticking out of a bottle of Blatz ("draft-brewed at local prices"), and two Pabst statues.

The Cascarelli Family has run a business at this corner since 1909. After the great "100 year flood" of 1908 destroyed his old store, Robert Cascarelli re-opened his cigar-candy-fruit store in the new 116 S. Superior location in January 1909. When Prohibition was lifted in 1933, Robert's sons Louis and Frank turned Cascarelli's into the pub we know today.

It all has the feel of warm longevity, with 8 old wooden booths for groups of friends and family, plenty of room for bellying up to the bar, nothing fancy, and with a happy hum to the place at 330PM on a Wednesday afternoon. According to waitress Nikki, sometime around the 70s, the Cascarellis bought the neighboring tavern to the north (further away from the corner), and knocked down the wall between the 2 pubs. The century-old back bar from the neighboring watering hole is still up, a good 20' long, and in great condition. Cascarelli's brings in occasional guitar pickers in addition to regular shows by the Albion College Jazz Ensemble (*"it's fun, it's jazz, it's pizza, it's Relli's!"*).

One constant since 1909 is Cascarelli's Peanuts: today, you can buy peanuts created from the same peanut roaster used by the family over 100 years ago. These cashews and redskin peanuts are ordered for shipment all over the world. Since 1970, Jim Cascarelli runs the bar, the 3rd generation of the family at the corner of Superior and Center in Albion. Jim and Nancy's kids are involved in the business, so the good news is this wonderful bar, a bar that your grandfather would feel at home in and you will, too, should be with us for a long, long time yet.

Chapter Sources: www.albion.edu, Christine Kosmowski - Calhoun County Water Resources Commissioner, www.mlive.com, www.d3football.com, GREAT (Grand River Environmental Action Team)

Kalamazoo River/ Western Michigan University

Degree of Paddling Difficulty: beginner friendly (level 1 of 3)

Livery: Lee's Adventure Sports, 311 W. Kilgore Road, Portage MI 49002; (269) 381-7700; www.leesadventuresports.com.

River Quote: "Age does not diminish the extreme disappointment of having a scoop of ice cream fall from the cone" – anonymous

Kalamazoo River Soundtrack: Pockets Full of Michigan – Squeaky Clean Cretins, The Kalamazoo River Song – Joe Reilly & the Woodward School Students, Up a Lazy River – Pete Fountain, Harbor Lights – Boz Scaggs, Great Gate of Kiev – WMU Brass Ensemble

Detroit Tigers radio affiliate: listen to WKZO 590AM to follow the Tigers when paddling the Kalamazoo near the WMU campus.

Directions to the launch site: I-94 West to exit 81/Business Loop 94; take Business Loop 94 to River Street and turn right/north; take River Street to Comstock Street, on the northern edge of the Kalamazoo River, and turn left. In 100', turn right into Merrill Park. The launch site is at the SW corner of River & Comstock. Restrooms available.

Directions to the take-out: I-94 West to exit 81/Business Loop 94; take Business Loop 94 to 43/Riverside Drive and turn right/north; take Riverside Drive to Patterson

Street and turn left/west; Verburg Park and its boat ramp on the bay will be on your left. Restrooms available.

Background of the Kalamazoo River:

The Kalamazoo Rivers runs west for 130 miles, from its headwaters at Albion's Rieger Park and flowing through Marshall, Battle Creek, and Kalamazoo until its Saugatuck river mouth. The 2010 Enbridge oil spill spread out along 40 miles of the river, effecting the Kalamazoo riverbed from Marshall in the east to Morrow Lake in the west, stopping just short of this chapter's Merrill Park to Verburg Park section of the river, where catches of walleye, catfish, and smallmouth bass are common. Wildlife viewed on today's trip includes deer, beavers, blue herons, turtles, and ducks; in an amusing sight, a turtle and a duck shared the same log.

Working to keep the waters of the Kalamazoo River watershed clean, as well as organizing and encouraging canoeing & kayaking recreational opportunities in the river, is the Kalamazoo River Watershed Council. The KRWC conducts an annual early-October river clean-up called *Krazy for the Kazoo* with volunteers at multiple locations along the river, from Albion to the east to Otsego in the west, clearing the water of debris and trash, planting trees and removing invasive species. Later each October, a second volunteer opportunity takes place, organized by the Kalamazoo River Guardians, a monitoring group that collects and identifies aquatic insects.

Among the recreational river activities the Kalamazoo River Watershed Council schedules are the *Kanoe the Kazoo* outings on Saturdays from May through October, including the "Lost Paddle". Co-sponsored with Lee's Adventure Sports and Arcadia Ales Brewing Co., the "Lost Paddle" covers the first 3 and one-half miles of the 4.2 mile trip outlined in this chapter, from the launch at Merrill Park in Comstock, running through the City of Kalamazoo, and taking out at Arcadia Brewing where music, prizes, food and beer awaits the Lost Paddle participants.

For information on all of the Kalamazoo River Watershed Council volunteer and recreational events, check their website at www.kalamazooriver.org.

Camping: Cold Brook County Park provides lodging in the nearby town of Climax. The 276 campground's acres covers 3 lakes (swimming beaches, fishing, boat ramps) and a wetlands, 14 rustic sites, 29 sites with electricity and water, restrooms, showers, picnic shelters, and hiking trails. Cold Brook County Park is located at 14467 East MN Avenue in Climax, MI 49034, phone 269-746-4270; www.kalcounty.com/parks/coldbrook/index.html

Paddling the Kalamazoo:

- Total trip 4.2 miles, 1 hour and 25 minutes (check with the livery for longer trip options).

- Merrill Park has a boat ramp, pavilion, bathrooms, basketball court, baseball diamond, & kids play area, while park benches line the river. Fishing is popular from the banks.

Launching at Merrill Park, the river flows from right to left (east to west). Across from the ramp an island with a miniature lighthouse marks the river split. Stay to the left of the split, through the rocks and rapids (visible from Merrill Park). *Suggestion:* from the ramp, paddle a few feet upstream (right and towards the River Street Bridge), so that when you turn to begin paddling the rapids, you have sufficient time to position your canoe/kayak through the river's center between the rocks on the left and on the right. The river from Merrill Park to Verburg Park has an average width of 60' – 100', and a depth that ranges from inches deep (at the Merrill Park rocky rapids) to, for the vast majority of the trip, over a paddle length. This chapter's trip was in April, when the water level was only slightly higher than "normal" conditions.

.5 mile/11 minutes: to the right, a lagoon sprawls below a pedestrian bridge of the *Kalamazoo River Valley Trail*, which runs along the river for most of this trip. The large orange structure beyond the left bank is the Tap House Lamplighter on Comstock Avenue, with multiple bars and a reception center, formerly a celery cold-storage unit.

.9 mile/20 minutes: pass below the Sprinkle Road Bridge. The bridge was built above a grassy island that stretches for one-tenth of a mile, upstream to downstream of the bridge. Visualize a cross created by the north-south bridge sitting above the west-east island.

1.3 miles/28 minutes: stay left as a narrow section of the river splits right; the right split courses through a concrete tunnel with stone supports below a Kalamazoo River Valley Trail pedestrian bridge. Downstream 200', the river split reconnects as a stream emerges from the forest on the right.

1.6 miles/32 minutes: on the left, a drainage ditch on the upstream edge of a paper pulp landfill emerges from a concrete tunnel, running beneath a pedestrian bridge with stone supports.

2.2 miles/42 minutes: pass below the M96/King Highway Bridge as the river makes a big bend right. Once past the bridge and to your right, watch for osprey families nesting on a once-used transformer within the old Georgia-Pacific property. Though a large platform was built, fitted with an osprey-cam, across the river to entice the ospreys away from the transformer and the Kalamazoo River Valley Trail below, this was only briefly successful (perhaps too shy for their reality TV debut via osprey-cam) and the families soon returned to their transformer nesting area. A Facebook page was created to monitor the ospreys: "Kalamazoo-Osprey-Family".

2.5 miles/48 minutes: paddling alongside the corrugated right-bank fence takes you through "echo valley" – just shout if you doubt.

2.7 mile/52 minutes: paddle below an old train trestle and then a Kalamazoo River Valley Trail pedestrian bridge. A dirt island left of midstream makes a fine location for a river break.

2.9 miles/56 minutes: behind the trees on the left is Mayor's Riverfront Park and Homer Stryker Field, home of the Kalamazoo Growlers minor league baseball team.

3.3 miles/1 hour and 2 minutes: pass below the Mills Street Bridge with the gently rolling terrain of the Red Arrow Golf Course to the left.

3.5 miles/1 hour and 10 minutes: paddle beneath the M43 Bridge as on the left the Kalamazoo River Valley Trail ducks under the bridge alongside you. The Arcadia Ales Brewery & Bar and its canoe/kayak launch is on the right bank past the bridge. Merging left is pretty Portage Creek.

3.9 miles/1 hour and 18 minutes: pass by the "City of Kalamazoo Park" sign on the left bank (at pavilion with tables) and then beneath Gull Road. Past Gull Road on the left is the upstream end of Verberg Park. The Kalamazoo River Valley Trail connects both parks.

As you pass beneath the Gull Road Bridge, you are only 2 minutes from your river exit...

4.1 miles/1 hour 20 minutes: Verberg Park bay widens on your left, although the passage from river to bay is narrow and easily missed. Paddle across the small bay to the boat ramp take-out.

4.2 miles/1 hour 25 minutes: you are in! at the Verburg Park boat ramp.

The Kalamazoo River crack research team: Olivia Vollmers, Gary "Mothman" Muir, Chris Muir, Yoshi Schlager, Heidi Hartland, Nancy Schlager, Jenine Urlich, Molly Lacy, Dennis Lacy, Glenn Isenhart, Nate Strong, Dan Burton, Jonnie Johnson, Ty Steffler, Kyak Ken, Maggie & Doc

The College: Western Michigan University

1903 W. Michigan Avenue, Kalamazoo MI 49008-5200, phone (269) 387-1000; www. wmich.edu

As we learned in the classic movie "Animal House", there is a little-known codicil in the Faber College constitution which gives the dean unlimited power to preserve order in time of campus emergency. However, an even _more_ obscure college fact is that the world's largest annual gathering of scholars specializing in medieval studies is hosted by Western Michigan University: the _International Congress on Medieval Studies_ takes place each May on WMU's Kalamazoo campus, attended on average by 3,000 scholars with the 50th such meeting taking place in 2015. As Emil Faber once said, "Knowledge is Good".

In 1903, Western State Normal School was established by act of the Michigan Legislature and opened by Dr. Dwight Waldo as a 2-year school for training teachers, the 4th such school in the state of Michigan (after Eastern, Central, and Northern). The school was soon restructured into a 4-year institute with the first Bachelor's degrees awarded in 1920. The school's name was changed in 1927 to Western State Teachers College, but what did not change was the nickname Western State was known as, a name that befits a school built on rolling hillsides: Hilltoppers. Western's nickname did not change from the Hilltoppers to the Broncos until 1939. Two years later, the Western Michigan Teachers College became known as the Western Michigan College of Education, shortened to Western Michigan College in 1955, and in 1957 finally renamed Western Michigan University.

WMU's campuses covers 1,289 acres serving 25,000 students. Michigan's 4th largest research university (classified as such by the Carnegie Foundation in 2000) includes the Kalamazoo main campus and Parkview campus, and campuses in Battle Creek, Benton Harbor, Grand Rapids, Lansing, Muskegon, Royal Oak and Traverse City. The WMU aviation campus at the W.K. Kellogg Airport in Battle Creek is considered to be one of the finest aviation campuses in the world. In addition to the Aviation College, Western's Academic colleges are in Arts & Sciences, Business, Education and Human Development, Engineering and Applied Sciences, Fine Arts, Health and Human Services, and the Graduate College. The programs offered by these colleges total 142 bachelors, 72 masters and 30 doctoral.

Many of these programs rank among the top of their kind in the USA. As a result, Western has gained both a national and an international reputation as one of the best places to study in aviation flight science, creative writing, engineering management technology, evaluation, experimental atomic physics, geology, integrated supply management, jazz studies, medieval studies, occupational therapy, paper engineering, psychology, sales and business marketing, and speech pathology. This recognition includes...

- For over 2 decades running, U.S. News & World Report has classified WMU among the nation's finest universities.

- The Princeton Review lists WMU on its annual online list of Best Midwestern Colleges.

- Military Times *EDGE* names WMU one of the country's best institutions for military veterans, and the only Michigan school to have appeared each year on the annual Best for Vets list.

- The Sustainable Endowments Institute green report card acknowledges WMU as one of only 3 Michigan universities to be included on the list of 80 USA "Campus Sustainability Leaders."

Through WMU's collaborative life science research and commercialization activities, over 30 students have been able to launch start-up companies. Another recent development was the 2014 opening of the WMU Homer Stryker M.D. School of Medicine, a collaborative effort of the university, philanthropists, and Kalamazoo's 2 world-class teaching hospitals, further boosting life sciences innovation and economic growth.

On top of all the academia, when you consider that the women's soccer team was the Mid- American Conference champions in 2003, 2013 and 2015, well the brown and gold is on a roll – go get 'em Broncos!

The Tavern #1: Arcadia Ales Brewing Company, 701 E. Michigan, Kalamazoo MI 49007; (269) 276-0458; http://www.arcadiaales.com/

Ok, I don't normally visit pubs quite as fancy as this one, but when folks are nice enough to build a tavern that you can paddle to (3.5 mile mark of this chapter's trip), it'd be rude not to at least stop by. Once on dry land, Arcadia's outdoor seating area gives you a sweet view of the Kalamazoo River, its merger with Portage Creek, and the gorgeous pedestrian bridge crossing over Portage Creek. The view from indoors is pretty good, too.

Arcadia opened in 2014 and part of their first year celebration was a canoe and kayak trip, with a major assist from Lee's Adventure Sports (our livery for this chapter's trip), for over 100 folks that ended at the brewery.

The grub cannot be ordered from your seat, as the kitchen is cafeteria-style. The vast majority of the food our paddling group ordered was given very high marks including the smoked pulled-pork sandwich, mac 'n cheese, ribs, and pork tacos. The wood-fired pizza will be a future meal.

The grog is all handcrafted, British-style, ales. While asking the waitress what Arcadia beer tastes closest to Pabst Blue Ribbon was an exercise in futility, I did enjoy one of their ales that was on tap, a fine brew called Cheap Date (the name a symbiotic connection to PBR). Arcadia described Cheap Date as "the perfect beer for spending time outside in the Spring... with this incredibly pale ale, Arcadia offers a highly session-able brew that entices your palate with a gentle balance of fine Pilsner malt, Citra Hops and a touch of lemon zest." This contrasted with how the folks at the next Kalamazoo River bar we visited, the Green Top Tavern, described Pabst Blue Ribbon beer: "it's available in a bottle". I'll be right there...

The Tavern #2: Green Top Tavern, 250 E Michigan Ave, Kalamazoo, MI 49007; (269) 342-5938; no, there's no website, ya durn whipper snapper!

Now we're talking. A true classic tavern in Kalamazoo's old Haymarket District, the Green Top has been in business since 1924. Coty Lee represents the 4th generation of ownership for his family. The Green Top has a beautiful back bar that makes you want to get on a bar stool and belly up, a well-stocked bar, 8 beers on tap, bottled beer including the afore mentioned PBR, a pool table if you're in the mood, a wall-sized Detroit Tiger schedule including today's whupping of the White Sox, 9 to 1 (Bless You Boys) that sits beneath a Pabst magnet in case you forgot what to order next. The excellent juke box was cranking out the classics that had the table talking about the virtues of AC DC to Led Zeppelin to the Vanilla Fudge and on and on and on.

The Green Top's menu includes munchies, sides, fish baskets, sandwiches, hot dogs, and burgers (voted best burger in Kalamazoo). The half-pound burgers were done exactly as requested and at an excellent value, about one-half the cost found at other pubs.

Oh yeah, and owner Coty was wearing a Tiger hat.

Chapter Sources: Dan Burton, Nate Strong, Kyak Ken Nesbitt, www.wmich.edu, Wikipedia

Kawkawlin River / Saginaw Valley State University

Degree of Paddling Difficulty: beginner (level 1 of 3)

Livery: Ike's Mobile Kayak; (989) 750-5251, www.ikeskayaks.com; Ike's also services the Pine (near Alma), the Chippewa, the Cedar, and the Kawkawlin rivers.

River Quote: "Because of her love of eating other people's food, she's been nicknamed *the Seagull*. If she's in a good mood, she'll ask if you're done" – Matthew Rose

Kawkawlin River Soundtrack: Lazy River – Chet Atkins & Les Paul, Saginaw Michigan – Lefty Frizzell, Rivers of the Hidden Funk – Joe Walsh, Cotton Fields – Chris Thomas King, Time Warp – Doctor Frank N. Furter

Detroit Tigers radio station: listen to WSGW 790AM to follow the Tigers when paddling the Kawkawlin near the Saginaw Valley State University campus.

Directions to the launch site: I-75 to exit 164/Wilder Road, go west on Wilder Road to Four Mile Road and turn right/north; take Four Mile Road to Wheeler Road; at the Four Mile and Wheeler intersection, and 50' west of I75, is the "Kawkawlin launch site" sign. No restrooms available.

- Chicago-style pizza bonus: on the way to the launch site, before heading west on Wilder Road, consider a brief detour and head east, and within a few feet there is an Uno Pizza on the left. Call ahead to pick one up for the river, (989) 684-8667.

Directions to the take-out: I-75 to exit 164/Wilder Road, right/east on Wilder for 2 miles to State Park Road and turn left/north. Take State Park Road for 2 miles and, immediately after crossing over the Kawkawlin River, the Castaways Bar appears. The take-out is a few feet to the west of the Castaways deck. Restrooms available.

Background of the Kawkawlin River:

The trip launch takes place on the Kawkawlin's 13-mile long south branch. The south branch headwaters are northeast of Midland, and it ends as it merges with the 36-mile long north branch to create the main branch, just upstream from the village of Kawkawlin. The relatively short main branch runs for 4.5 miles until it empties into Saginaw Bay. The fishing is good on the Kawkawlin for northern pike, round gobies, walleye, perch, and largemouth bass.

Making the Kawkawlin a better place for all of us is the Kawkawlin River Watershed Association. The KRWA organizes an annual river clean-up, installs kayak/canoe launch sites, helps with the rail trail, and works on river restoration & water quality projects. To view their current efforts and to see how you can help, check out the KRWA website at www.kawkawlinriver.com.

Camping: 10 minutes to the southeast of the trip take-out is Finn Road Park. Situated on the shores of Saginaw Bay, Finn Road Park is both a campground and a boat launch. Each site includes water, electric, sewer hook-ups, picnic table, and fire pit. Known for their walleye fishing, the park amenities include a pavilion, bath house, and nature trails. Finn Road Park is located at 2300 North Finn Rd., Essexville MI 48732, ph. 989-894-0055; www.finnroadpark.com.

Paddling the Kawkawlin River:

- Total trip 5.1 miles, 2 hours (check with livery for other paddling options)

The launch is 200' west of the south-bound lanes of I-75. The river here is 2' deep and 30' wide with tall cattails on each side of you and even taller cattails just ahead. I-75 traffic visible from the launch includes many vehicles with canoes & kayaks on the roofs, a sight good for the soul.

This 2 hour journey provides two distinct experiences: part 1 is the initial 45 minutes, through fields of cattails, herons flying all around, and the water 75% covered with seaweed (note that this trip was taken in July; crack researchers Steve and Glenn experienced zero seaweed during an April paddle). With each paddle stroke, the blade emerges from the river weighed down with seaweed cover... to minimize this, keep your strokes close to the surface, skimming the river top; Part 2 on the river is the remaining 1 hour and 15 minutes, as the river widens, deepens, and flows alongside a series of homes and boat docks & launches.

15 minutes from launch, tag alder bushes mingle with the cattails on the riverbanks. At this point, 100'-150' beyond the cattails, a forest of maple and oak trees tower.

.9 miles/24 minutes: the first homes seen today, 100 yards beyond the right bank.

1 mile/27 minutes: as the river bends left, the seaweed slowly begins to dissipate. The river has deepened from 2' at the launch to 4'.

1.2 miles/34 minutes: the first feeder creek, 3' wide, merges from your right.

1.5 miles/45 minutes: the North Branch of the Kawkawlin, 15' wide at its mouth, emerges from the left. At this point, the north and south branches merge to form the start of the Main Branch of the Kawkawlin River.

With the merger of the north and south branches, the seaweed varies from a non-factor to non-existent, while the cattails are now only spotty on the left shore and completely replaced by bushes and forests on the right. The extra volume of the north branch has doubled the width of the Kawkawlin River to 60' and the depth to over 6'.

1.8 miles/51 minutes: preceded by a merging creek, H.H. Stein Memorial Park sits on the right. The park, located on the south side of the village of Kawkawlin, includes a grassy boat launch.

2 miles/55 minutes: paddle below Old Beaver Road, reminding one of a Martin Short story told about a visit to Bea Arthur's dressing room...

2.2 miles/59 minutes: to your right, "Ed and Mary Ann's" place includes an enormous stump of a double-trunk tree.

2.3 miles/1 hour: after paddling alongside the right shore home displaying a windmill, pass beneath M13. Riverside homes now populate the banks in large numbers.

2.6 miles/1 hour 5 minutes: on the left, a home sits above a metal sea wall and 3 tiers of railroad ties, an impressive effort to stave off property erosion. Downstream, a 200' long wooden sea wall continues the effort.

2.9 miles/1 hour and 13 minutes: the fine looking brown A-frame on your left sits beyond a wooden sea wall; among many riverside beauties, this one stands out.

3.1 miles/1 hour and 16 minutes: a dead creek merges on a severe diagonal from the left, its banks home to 2 homes visible from the Kawkawlin.

3.3 miles/1 hour and 20 minutes: christened the "crusty old weeping willow" by Glenn, on your right the tall & ancient willow weeps with an unusual-looking dimpled trunk.

The dramatic increase in the number of pontoon boats, with a sprinkling of speed boats, boat docks, and boat launches, testify to the water depth of an estimated 12'.

3.6 miles/1 hour and 26 minutes: JJ refers to the red brick home on the left as the "mayor's house", due in part to the white & blue bunting draped over the 2nd floor balcony, the ideal venue from which to deliver political speeches ("I will not allow my unfortunate incarceration to derail future service to my constituents").

4.1 miles/1 hour and 36 minutes: paddling below Euclid Avenue/Highway 247, the cottonwood tree (with the power lines running through it) on the downstream side of the bridge and to your right, is letting a cotton storm loose. It's snowing in July!

4.6 miles/1 hour and 44 minutes: a very large creek merges from the left, with homes on both of its banks and on its shores sea walls, pontoon boats, and canoes & kayaks.

5.1 miles/2 hours: you are in! at the Castaways Bar take-out on the left; a few feet upstream from the Castaways back deck, look for the stairs marked "kayak access" alongside the twin rails used to pull your canoe or kayak from the water to dry land.

Kawkawlin River Crack Research Team: Glenn Isenhart, Steve Arnosky, JJ Johnson, Bob Strange, and Doc

The College: Saginaw Valley State University

7400 Bay Rd, University Center MI 48710, phone 989-964-4000; www.svsu.edu.

For one who had never before visited the Saginaw Valley State University campus, viewing the gorgeous landscape is quite a sweet surprise. Arguably, the most outstanding campus feature is a toss-up between the Marshall M. Fredericks Sculpture Museum & Garden and Founders Hall...

The Marshall M. Fredericks Sculpture Museum & Garden includes 200 works created by the internationally-known and Detroit-based sculptor, Marshall M. Fredericks. Located at the Arbury Fine Arts Center, Fredericks' art displayed outdoors cause an involuntary action by anyone driving through the campus to immediately pull the car over, get out, and go for a stroll among the works. The "Black Elk" piece, displaying a Native American warrior struck by a spear while astride a buffalo, is mesmerizing. In 1988, ten years before his passing, Fredericks chose SVSU as the place to display his work, a wonderful gift.

Similarly, the beauty of Founders Hall pulls you towards it. A quaint pedestrian bridge over a stone creek takes you through the trees and into the open landscape where this fascinating wooden architecture lies. Even standing inside gives the feeling of being surrounded by nature as the A-frame hall features floor to ceiling windows that look out over the unique tableau. It is the good fortune of Saginaw Valley State U. students, staff, alumni, and their families that this stunning hall may be used for their reunions, weddings, or other gatherings. As a nice bonus, one of Marshall M. Fredericks' sculptured works greets visitors just a few feet from the main Founders Hall entrance.

SVSU is the youngest of Michigan's 15 public colleges and universities, having celebrated its 50th anniversary in 2013. On November 13, 1963, the State Board of Education approved the creation of Saginaw Valley College. Dr. Sam Marble, the college's first president, was the driving force in raising the $4M needed to acquire a site to begin campus construction. The college name was changed to Saginaw Valley State College in 1974 and then in 1987 to Saginaw Valley State University.

Saginaw Valley State has student enrollment of 10,000 on a campus of 782 acres. The school's undergraduate and graduate programs are under 5 colleges: Arts & Behavioral Sciences, Business & Management, Education, Nursing & Health Services, and Science, Engineering & Technology. SVSU's most popular majors include Registered Nursing, Criminal Justice, Social Work, Pre-Med, and Business Administration. Students may choose from over 70 programs of study that lead to one of ten bachelor degrees, or one of 12 graduate programs (11 master's degree and one doctoral program).

Among the fun facts at Saginaw Valley State University, home of the Cardinals...

- The year 2000 presidential campaign of George W. Bush brought the candidate to the campus just days before becoming elected President.

- In 2009, SVSU alum Tony Ceccacci was director in charge of the mission to repair the Hubble Space Telescope.

- SVSU's residential facilities have been voted "Michigan's Best Residential Life" by the Michigan Organization of Residence Halls Association (MORHA).

- Ming Chuan University, the first Asian university to be accredited in the United States, opened their Michigan Campus in SVSU's Gilbertson Hall in 2014.

- The Carnegie Foundation for the Advancement of Teaching bestowed upon SVSU its *2015 Community Engagement Classification*, acknowledging a "partnership of university knowledge & resources with those of the public & private sectors to enrich scholarship, research, and creative activity; enhance curriculum, teaching and learning; prepare educated, engaged citizens; strengthen democratic values and civic responsibility; address critical societal issues; and contribute to the public good". The designation is in effect for 10 years.

And then there was the 1979 Rocky Horror Picture Show riot. In December of 1979, 250 Saginaw Valley students attended a campus holiday showing of the 1975 cult classic. The rice that Rocky Horror movie-goers traditionally throw at the screen during the wedding scene was instead kept in the big plastic bags it came in and thrown as heavy projectiles at other audience members. Suddenly, the scene exploded into a full-blown food fight and beyond, quickly escalating into flying salt 'n pepper shakers and even a few chairs. When the movie was stopped, the rascals merely moved outdoors between the dorms, pelting each other with squirt guns and snowballs – all good fun until someone woke up the county sheriff with a hoax phone call, telling him that "150 Iranian students had taken over the campus and destroyed a building" (note that this was one month after the U.S. Embassy employees had been taken hostage by Iranian radicals in Tehran).

Soon, the midnight darkness was broken by a long line of flashing blue lights in the distance, vehicles bringing police in riot helmets carrying night sticks. While some students departed quickly, many now directed their snowballs at the police as others opened their dorm room windows to jeer the cops – and that's how 53 students ended up in jail, including the star quarterback of the football team. The quarterback used his one call to phone football head coach and Athletic Director Frank "Muddy" Waters, who showed up to bail his player out. The university posted bond ($1,025 total) for the incarcerated 45 who had not been bailed out by parents or the football coach, and those kids were transported in vans back to campus the following morning.

As the *Saginaw News* noted the next day, "officers swept onto the campus amid rumors of Iranian involvement and calls picturing a building under siege" to illustrate how the situation escalated as it did. Although subsequent hearings would find reason to suspend two students from the dorms and one from the college, many others would receive letters of apology from the school's administration. T-shirts reading, "I SURVIVED THE SVSC RIOT" became popular on campus, as did the 53 students who were briefly jailed.

The Tavern: Castaways Food and Spirits, 3940 Boy Scout Road, Bay City MI 48706; (989) 686- 3558; www.castawaysbaycity.com.

They have a deck sign for Rolling Rock beer, but they don't have Rolling Rock beer. However, since this **is** a bar located on a river, a tavern that you can paddle right up to, all is forgiven. Whether operating under previous names Salays, Maxey's, Low Tide, Captain Jake's, or today's Castaways, this is the right business at the right place.

Out of 75 or so Michigan rivers, there are few that you can, or could, paddle right up to a tavern on... the Thirsty Sturgeon (old Meadows) on the Sturgeon, Fresh Booze on the Rouge (alas, now gone) on the Rouge, Brewster's on the Rocky, Duke's Canoe Club on the Looking Glass, Brady's Bar on the Boardman, and in the U.P. the Ford River Pub on the Ford & Andy's Seney Bar (*some get there by canoe, some get there by car*) on the Fox. There may be some others, but the point is what the Castaways offers is a rare treat for paddlers: the chance to take a grub 'n grog break while paddling a river.

Although canoe paddles have been incorporated into the indoors décor (a cool look), outside of using the bathroom OR taking cover from the elements, out on the deck is where you want to be at the Castaways. Hold on there, we see a help-yourself popcorn machine next to the indoor bar... grab a basket of popcorn before returning to the deck.

The food consumed by our crack research team members was well-reviewed: the Island Burger, the Walleye Sandwich (aka the Giant Fish Sandwich; fish is what the tavern is best known for), Reuben, fries, homemade tavern chips, homemade brick oven pizza, and - although we did not order one - "the World's Largest Stromboli": ordered by someone at an adjacent table and per waitri Alexi a big seller, "the World's Largest Stromboli" had a *no brag, just fact*, look about it.

With Saginaw Bay only 1 mile away, boaters come from all over the area to dine and drink at the Castaways, including from AuGres, Standish, Pinconning, and all parts of Bay City. During our meal, we talked of future Kawkawlin River trips, maybe launching at H.H. Stein Memorial Park, today's 51 minute mark, paddling the 1 hour and 10 minutes to the Castaways, stopping for a brew before continuing on for the 1 mile to Saginaw Bay, then turning to paddle back to the Castaways, to cap a off the trip with a meal on the deck. The planning cannot be stopped, it can only be contained (just a little).

Chapter Sources: www.baycounty-mi.gov, Alexi at the Castaways, www.mybaycity. com, www.svsu.edu, Wikipedia

Macatawa River / Hope College

Degree of Paddling Difficulty: skilled (level 3 of 3) due to the potentially choppy waters at the eastern end of Macatawa Lake at trip's end.

Livery: Kayak-Kayak, 1200 Ottawa Beach Road, Holland MI 49424; (616) 366-1146, www.kayak-kayak.com. Kayak Kayak's owner is Skip Nagelvoort who also services the Pigeon, the Black, and the Kalamazoo rivers.

River Quote: "I am calmed by still waters and grateful for the simple pleasure of being on the water" – Skip Nagelvoort

Macatawa River Soundtrack: Into the Blue – Boney James, By This River – Brian Eno, the Windmill Song – Tom Curtain, Tiptoe Through the Tulips – Tiny Tim, Playful Pizzicato – Hope College Orchestra

Detroit Tigers radio affiliate: listen to WHTC 1450AM to follow the Tigers when paddling the Macatawa near the Hope College campus.

Directions to the launch site: Paw Paw Park is at 270 S. River Road in Holland. From downtown Holland, take Chicago Road/Business 196 East to 112th Street (Crown Motors is at the SW corner) and turn right. As soon as you cross over the river, turn right into the park, look for the launch on your right. Restrooms available.

Directions to the take-out: Dunton Park is located at 290 Howard Avenue in Holland. From downtown Holland, take River Avenue north and cross over the Macatawa River. Turn left on Douglas, left on Jefferson, right on Howard and go past the Michigan State University building, turn in left at the "Holland Princess dinner cruises" sign. The take-out access is at the east end of the park, the restrooms are on the west end. Restrooms available.

Background of the Macatawa River:

The "People of the Three Fires", the Native American Ottawas, Chippewas and Potawatomi tribes who inhabited this area, named the river the "Muck-i-ta-wog-go-me", meaning "black water". The Macatawa, a corruption of "Muck-i-ta-wog-go-me", also goes by the name Black River, which can be a bit confusing since there is another Black River (running from Bangor to South Haven) 30 minutes to the south of the Macatawa River. The headwaters of the 16-mile long Macatawa River form east of the town of Holland and southeast of the I-196 expressway. From there, the river flows northwest then west until it empties into Lake Macatawa near Lake Michigan. Anglers have had great success reeling in carp and walleye from the Macatawa River.

A steward of the Macatawa River and its surroundings is the *Macatawa Watershed Project*. The MWP was created in 1999 to combat the high levels of phosphorus entering Lake Macatawa, the end point of this chapter's trip. The group's stated goal is to reduce the lake phosphorus by 70%. Most phosphorus gets into the water when rain runs off the surface of the land, carrying fertilizer, manure, and other organic wastes into the rivers and lakes. The resultant algae grows faster than ecosystems can handle it, harming water quality, food resources & habitats, and decreasing the oxygen that fish & other aquatic life need to survive. The Macatawa Watershed Project, through public awareness, education, & using best management practices, works with the local community to reduce the phosphorus impact to Lake Macatawa. To learn more about the MWP, go to their website at www.the-macc.org/watershed/overview.

Camping: Lake Macatawa Campground is a 10 minute drive from the Dunton Park take-out, near where Lake Macatawa and Lake Michigan meet. Sitting within the Holland State Park, the Lake Macatawa Campground offers 211 campsites with fire pits and picnic tables. Their address is 2215 Ottawa Beach Road in Holland MI 49424, ph. 616-399-9390; www.michigan.org/property/lake-macatawa-campground.

Paddling the Macatawa River:

- Total trip 3.7 miles, 1 hour and 40 minutes (check the livery website for other river trips)

- NOTE: once you paddle below the River Avenue Bridge, the river gradually grows more challenging as you encounter the westerly winds (12 - 15 knot wind is common) blowing in from Lake Michigan, creating choppy, unsteady, water and whitecaps. In addition, large boats/industrial barges and their wakes frequent the lake. Only experienced paddlers – with their life vests on! - should continue downstream from River Avenue.

There are two launch site options at Paw Paw Park: the first is between a parking area and, only 30' away, the river. If the river water level is low (during this early-May trip, river levels were slightly above average, high enough to launch here) there may be a severe drop off from land to water. If that is the case, you may want to walk your boats about 100' or so downstream to the gentle slope leading to the river's edge. At the launch, the river is about 40' wide.

.3 mile/7 minutes: paddle beneath the Business 196 Bridge. The next bridge you pass below is the 120th Avenue/Waverly Road Bridge. Beyond this bridge you see today's first homes and a blue pavilion on the left shore.

1.4 miles/35 minutes: the Highway 131 Bridge. 100' upstream from the bridge, a creek merges from the right. In the creek lives dozens of turtles and a debris field wall 30 yards from the river effectively blocking further exploration.

1.6 miles/39 minutes: a ghost bridge spans the river, where a grass road leads to the water on both the left and right banks. Recent shoreline activity includes fires built where the road meets the river.

1.9 miles/47 minutes: guarded by 3 turtles on a river branch, a big creek rolls in from the left. Downstream a railroad trestle crosses the river.

Windmill Island ahead!

2 miles/50 minutes: just beyond the railroad trestle the river bends right; on the left shore a tall rusted seawall, with large rocks at its base, signal the eastern edge of Windmill Island.

Just past Windmill Island's 2nd brick structure a break in the seawall on the left indicates a canal through which you paddle to the Island's center. This journey through Windmill Island is wonderful and the most outstanding feature of today's paddle. Tulip gardens grace both riverbanks, flags of many countries flutter in the breeze, with the Windmill itself on the right shore.

2.2 miles/58 minutes: you are right alongside the Windmill (to access the Island by vehicle: from downtown take 9th Street east to Lincoln Avenue, turn left/north and follow the signs).

2.4 miles/1 hour and 7 minutes: the western edge of Windmill Island supports a porta john and a canoe landing on the right (Skip informed us that you could also take-out on the left shore before passing the windmill). Just beyond, the main body of the river flows in from the right - paddle to the left at this merger. Big, beautiful homes inhabit the river's far bank. The Macatawa River at this point widens to a maximum of 300'.

3.1 miles/1 hour and 25 minutes: paddle below River Ave. Make sure your life vest is secured for the balance of this trip. You will commonly run into unsettled whitewater between the River Avenue Bridge and the take-out.

3.4 miles/1 hour and 30 minutes: you're directly between a factory beyond the left shore and an Upjohn plant beyond the right. The story goes that the Upjohn facility once produced Viagra and ended up dumping much product waste into the river. Since then, the carp are particularly spirited, jumping out of the river frequently.

3.7 miles/1 hour and 40 minutes: you are in! At the eastern end of Macatawa Lake, paddle just beyond the long wooden walkway that juts out into the lake, and turn towards the sandy beach on the right shore.

Macatawa River Crack Research Team: Kim VerMerris, Perry VerMerris, Bernadette Kearns, Chris Weaks, Eric Long, Maggie and Doc.

The College: Hope College

141 E. 12th Street, Holland MI 49422-9000, phone 616-395-7860; www.hope.edu

In 1898, a tug-of-war took place between Hope College students, facing off from each other across the Macatawa River. This annual Hope student body tug-of-war, missed only 4 years since 1898, is called "The Pull". The longest tug-of-war in "The Pull" series took place in 1977, lasting 3 hours and 51 minutes. In 1978, a rule change was implemented, limiting the event to 3 hours (the winner declared by a judge measuring the land gained). To quote John Lennon, "I got blisters on my fingers!"

121

22 years after the intramural exploits of "The Pull" first took place, another Hope athletic contest began, this one pitting Hope College students against students from outside of the institute: in the 1920-1921 basketball season, Hope defeated Calvin College by a score of 31 to 13, launching one of the greatest rivalries in college athletics. From the 1920-1921 through the 2014-2015 seasons (and a total of 191 basketball games played)...

- Hope leads the series by 98 to 93 over Calvin.

- The scoring difference between the 2 teams is less than one-half of a point (.304) per game in favor of Hope. Hope has scored 12,989 points, an average of 68.005 per game while Calvin has scored 12,931 points, an average of 67.702 per game. In other words, after 191 games, the two teams are separated by only 58 points.

- After the 1968-1969 season, Hope held a 16-win advantage in the series. Calvin won the next 22 games to go ahead in the series by six games. Since then, the series lead has exchanged hands five times: 1985-86 Hope, 1989-90 Calvin, 2006-07 Hope, 2006-07 Calvin and 2007-08 Hope.

- ESPN has identified the Hope-Calvin rivalry as among the greatest in college basketball, tops in NCAA Division III and fourth in all of collegiate hoops (based

122

on a poll of fans and ESPN's "panel of experts"): #1 - Duke vs. North Carolina, #2 - Connecticut vs. Tennessee (women), #3 - Louisville vs. Kentucky, #4 - Hope vs. Calvin. ESPN called Hope vs. Calvin "a great, under-the-radar college sports rivalry, unique in the approach both fans and players take to the game. While everyone is excited for tip-off, the rivalry doesn't carry the animosity that's usually found when two schools compete so closely for so long."

In 1846, Dutch immigrants left their Rotterdam homes in the country of Holland, taking 47 days to cross the Atlantic Ocean until landing in New York. From New York, the group of 60 traveled west led by the Reverend Albertus C. Van Raalte, who intended to buy land for a settlement in the Wisconsin Territory. An early winter forced the immigrants to seek shelter in Detroit, short of their Wisconsin goal. Talk was that good land was available on the western shore of the infant state of Michigan, resulting in the Dutch folk settling on the banks of Lake Macatawa in February of 1847, creating the beginnings of Holland, Michigan.

To meet the educational needs of this new Holland, the "Pioneer School" was built in 1851. If this new school would have been state-supported, it could not have had the Christian emphasis that Van Raalte desired, and it was arranged that the Pioneer School would be funded by the Reformed Church of America. In 1862, the school name was changed to the Holland Academy, and for the first time enrolled a college class in addition to elementary and secondary. In 1866, the institute received its Michigan state charter, becoming Hope College, the name honoring Reverend Van Raalte's belief that the early Pioneer School was, "the anchor of hope for this people in the future".

Hope College is a private, liberal arts school, situated on a campus gorgeous in large part due to the respect and maintenance of buildings over a century old. Sitting above campus on one of the town's only hills is the oldest building at Hope, Van Vleck Hall, built in 1857 of brick and stone. In the 1850s, the campus revolved around the 3-story tall structure, housing the classrooms, the library, and Hope's first president. Still the center of campus, Van Vleck Hall today serves as a women's residence hall. Another Hope building over a century old that gives the campus so much of its charm is Graves Hall. Built in 1894 to house a new library and chapel needed for the growing student body, today Graves is as stunning as ever and home to 5 classrooms, the 163-seat Winants Auditorium, the Presidents' Room, a conference room containing portraits of all of the college's presidents, the ground level Children's After School Achievement (CASA) and Upward Bound programs, and the Schoon Meditation Chapel.

Dimnent Memorial Chapel may be the most attention-grabbing building on the Hope College campus. Opened in 1929, the spectacular Gothic structure contains stained glass windows imported from Italy and France, a hand-carved pulpit constructed of solid rosewood, and its cornerstone is engraved with the college motto, *Spera in Deo*: Hope in God. Originally named Hope Memorial Chapel, and built when Hope's enrollment was only 434 students, it has seats for 1,500.

2015 marks 150 years since Hope College received its state charter. Enrollment today exceeds 3,300 students. Hope offers specialized study in more than 80 majors, minors and pre-professional programs, all of which lead to a Bachelor of Arts, Bachelor of Music, Bachelor of Science, Bachelor of Science in Engineering, or Bachelor of Science in Nursing degree.

The Princeton Review has recognized Hope as one of the most environmentally responsible colleges in the USA and Canada, while the Association of American Colleges has ranked Hope College's Phelps Scholars Program among only 32 USA institutions with an exemplary-rated diversity program in higher education.

"Fight on you big Dutchmen/Defend the Orange and Blue/Be strong and mighty/And shout out your loyalty/GO HOPE!/Fight on you big Dutchmen/Defend the Orange and Blue/Be Strong, Be True, and Mighty too/And come up with a Victory"

The Tavern #1: Beechwood Inn/Coyote Café Bar & Grill; 380 Douglas Avenue; Holland MI 49424; (616) 396-2355; www.bwoodinn.com.

The bar is a 10-minute walk from Dunton's Park. Take Howard Street west to Jackson Street, turn right on Jackson Street to Douglas Road where you turn left (west). The Beechwood Inn/ Coyote Café Bar & Grill will be on your left.

As Maggie observed, you have a mecca to retreat to after your time on the Macatawa River: Beechwood/Coyote Bar on the south side of Douglas, a few feet east of the bar is deBoer Bakkerij, known as one of the finest bakeries in the Midwest, and across Douglas from both is Captain Sundae for ice cream goodness.

The Beechwood/Coyote serves Pabst Blue Ribbon beer in bottles, so we're off to an excellent start. The food critiques by the crack research team ranged from two "not bads" to very high praise for, among others, the Bavarian Style Pub Burgers (char-grilled w/ melted cheddar on a grilled bakery pretzel bun topped with drunken onions – mm, mm good including the onions, and I don't care for onions), the Hillbilly Fries (w/ pulled pork, peppers, and mustard aioli), and fresh smelt, along with the always fine Henry Weinhart Root Beer.

The tavern has a very comfortable feel with an interesting back and front bar of corrugated metal, along with seating outside. Before the 1974 purchase of the bar by current owner Craig Butler, a bar called Jacks inhabited the building. On a winter 1982-1983 night, a car couldn't negotiate the big curve on the road in front of the bar, slammed into the Beechwood, exploded and burned the place down. Craig said it took 3 months to rebuild, but believes that he ended up with an even better tavern and restaurant, the one you enjoy today.

The Tavern #2: Curragh Irish Pub, 73 E. 8th Street (at College), Holland MI 49423; (616) 393-6340; www.curraghholland.com

Old country wisdoms adorns the walls of this classic downtown Irish tavern...

"Getting bad advice is one thing, taking it is a serious mistake", "A man who can't laugh at himself should be given a mirror", "Better the coldness of a friend than the sweetness of an enemy", "Irish blessing: when you slide down the bannister of life, may the splinters never point the wrong way".

This is not a shot 'n a beer bar that we so often seek after a day on the water. Two fellows from Chicago sunk $3M into the Curragh, enough money to keep several fraternities awash in Pabst Blue Ribbon beers and nightly pizzas from freshman year through alumni gatherings. Fancier than our tastes, but a very nice piece of Ireland indeed, highlighted with Celtic music (and blues 'n rock) played on the weekends.

Curragh's offers a complete menu of traditional Irish cuisine but, since we'd just partaken of the Beechwood Pub menu (see tavern #1), we settled for sharing a bread pudding dessert, so rich and sooooo delicious, and the best I've ever had. The beer list has Irish classics Guinness, Smithwick's, Harp, and Kilkenny, along with Michigan Drafts, British Beers, European Drafts, American Drafts, Draft Ciders, and good old bottled beers like Corona, Heineken, and Michelob.

Curragh's is located in the middle of Holland's downtown activity and is a short walk from the campus of Hope College. It's also directly across the street from a brewery, the Holland Brewing Company, and its' New Holland Pub on 8th.

The finest wall sign at Curragh's required translation: "Ceoil agus ol at Curragh" = "Drink, music, and fun at Curragh's!"

Chapter Sources: Skip Nagelvoort, www.the-macc.org/watershed/overview, www.hope.edu

Muskegon River / Ferris State University

Degree of Paddling Difficulty: beginner (level 1 of 3)

Livery: Sawmill Canoe Livery, 226 Baldwin Street, Big Rapids MI 49307; (231) 796-6408; www.sawmillbr.com

River Quote: "There's some bottom-skimming, but not enough to knock your beer over" – Yoshi **Bonus River Quote:** "Eagles may soar, but weasels don't get sucked into jet engines" – Steven Wright

Muskegon River Soundtrack: Madman Across the Water – Elton John, Southwest Floatage (the Muskegon River song) – Richard Bandlow & Stephen Goodfellow, Telecommunications – Flock of Seagulls, Calling Captain Autumn – Haircut 100, Little Gate's Special – Ferris State Jazz Band

Detroit Tigers radio stations: listen to WBRN 95.1FM/107.7FM/1460AM to follow the Tigers when paddling the Muskegon River near the Ferris State University campus.

Directions to the launch site: from Big Rapids, take Business US131/Northland Road north; where Bus. US131 turns left/west, stay straight north on Northland Rd.; shortly after Northland Rd. passes the 22 Mile Rd. intersection, turn right at the Paris Park sign. Restrooms available.

Directions to the take-out: from Big Rapids, take Business US131/Northland Road north to Pere Marquette Street and turn right/east; cross over the Muskegon River and, just past the Sawmill Canoe Livery, turn left/north on to Trestle Bend Drive/4th Avenue; after a short drive, Northend Riverside Park will be on the left. Restrooms available.

Background of the Muskegon River:

The 230 mile long Muskegon River is the 2nd longest river in Michigan, with only the 260 mile Grand River longer. The Muskegon's headwaters flow out of Houghton Lake, and from there it meanders in a generally southwest direction. The river's journey ends as it drifts into Muskegon Lake and through the mile long channel connecting Muskegon Lake to Lake Michigan. Its waters are best known by anglers for king salmon, brown trout, and its excellent fall steelhead run.

As the Muskegon River flows through Big Rapids, it is about midway between its Houghton Lake headwaters and its Lake Michigan river mouth. The section of the river outlined in this chapter runs from north to south, is wide and shallow, well-populated with rocks 2' and 3' in diameter scattered on the river floor, and blessed with banks full of gorgeous weeping willow trees.

An excellent steward of the river is the Muskegon River Watershed Assembly. In many of the communities that the river flows through, the MRWA organizes and participates in clean-up events each year, motivating local residents to volunteer their time and effort through the adopt-a-stream programs. Assembly activities include water quality monitoring, tree planting, removal of invasive species, and restoration of riparian areas (areas bordering rivers and streams). The MRWA also organizes canoeing & kayaking trips throughout the watershed each year, including their 2011 "Voyage of Discovery", an 11-day paddle of the entire length of the Muskegon River. If you'd like to be involved with a MRWA trip, a river clean-up or other project, or just interested in seeing what they are doing to make the Muskegon a better place for us all, check out their website at www.mrwa.org.

Camping: Paris Park, the launch site for this trip, is a fine campground on the banks of the river. There are 68 shaded sites, 3 rental cabins, 2 ponds, and picnic areas spread among the park's 40 wooden acres. Each of the 68 sites has a fire pit, picnic table, and hook-ups for electricity and water. Sand volleyball, horseshoes, a playground, paths through the woods, and access to the walking/hiking/biking White Pine Trail are part of the Paris Park fun.

The park is located at 22090 Northland Drive (see previous page for *"Directions to the launch site"*), Paris MI 49338, 231-796-3420; www.mecostacountyparks.com/paris

Paddling the Muskegon River:

- Total trip 5 miles, 1 hour and 55 minutes (check livery website for 1 hour to 7 day trips)

For the book, this section of the Muskegon was paddled in July and again in October – there was little difference in river depth in either month. Departing from the Paris Park launch, you're immediately paddling through a shallow and rocky riverbed, experiencing bottom-scraping, with larger rocks partially visible above the water's surface. The river is an estimated 120' wide.

.4 mile/10 minutes: a pine A-frame above a man-made waterfall makes a fine sight on the left shore. A few feet downstream, white water wraps around two islands where the deepest channel runs far right (important to note when river levels are low).

.7 mile/15 minutes: arrive at Bridge Street/Hoover Road, the 1st of two bridges on today's journey. Just beyond the bridge, a majestic weeping willow tree is on the right bank. 3 minutes downstream, another beautiful pine A-frame sits beyond the left bank. 2 minutes after the A-frame, pass by two midstream islands where the deepest water runs left. A muskrat dives into the river.

Fishermen near the shore say they're catching smallmouth bass and suckers, but the most impressive fishing happens midstream right in front of the canoe: a chocolate-brown, juvenile eagle suddenly swoops down, skimming over the river's surface, then streaks into the sky with its talons wrapped around an unfortunate fish, lighting with its catch on a branch 50' above the riverbank.

.9 mile/17 minutes: at the upstream end of a long island, a small creek rolls in from the right. The island lies slightly right of midstream.

1.3 miles/24 minutes: a fine-looking, octagonal-shaped, home is beyond the left shore. The river here runs 2' deep. Hard to see, but not to hear, a small 'n pretty waterfall drops down into the Muskegon on the right.

1.8 miles/32 minutes: two neighboring islands both host fine break spots, upstream sand and stone aprons with gentle slopes. 3' diameter rocks now occasionally poke their heads 2' above the water line. Deer are seen running through the brush a few feet beyond the right shore.

2 miles/38 minutes: amid a stand of birch on the left bank is a yellow home with a large garden.

2.4 miles/43 minutes: long white home with a green tin roof sits beyond the right bank, the start of several homes visible on the right. A deck 15' above the river creates an interesting visual, poking out from the surrounding trees and giving the impression that the deck is suspended alone in mid-air above the water (until you paddle close enough to see its accompanying home).

2.7 miles/48 minutes: a long, shallow (bottom-skimming to 6" deep) stretch spans the entire width of the river; stay right for the deepest channel and through water with a fun chop to it. In two minutes you reach the upstream end of a 200' long island, left of midstream, where the river deepens to 2'. At the end of the island and on the left, 2 grand weeping willow trees sway next to a white home, while across the river an old farm house sports a silo.

3.5 miles/1 hour: the several minutes of paddling through the fun chop in the river ends as the water deepens to 3'. Blue herons soar above in the distance at tree top level. A hill rises beyond the right bank, at its crest sits 4 homes. After passing by these homes you encounter a 150' long midstream island. Turtles sun themselves on large rocks protruding above the river surface.

3.8 miles/1 hour and 7 minutes: in the middle of the river, purple wild flowers populate a pretty little (50' long x 20' wide) island with large rocks at its upstream base. The wild flowers were a summer time treat during our July paddle, the purple bloom turned brown by our October visit.

Several minutes downstream, a tiny creek flows into the Muskegon; to the left, 11 wooden pilings support a ghost dock that once was. Geese enjoy the river in large numbers. A small island left of midstream brims with purple wild flowers (during our July paddle only, the bloom gone in October).

4.6 miles/1 hour 20 minutes: encounter a midstream island, 200' before the bridge. Paddle to the left of the island for a fine sandy break spot, 70' before the bridge, on the left bank. Continue on and pass below the 2nd of 2 bridges on today's trip, this one a railroad trestle. Once under the bridge, a gorgeous red home with white trim sits on the left with – lookout! – a huge midstream rock in front of the red house.

An impressively long run of wooden pilings along the right bank, and a shorter run of pilings on the left, support long-gone docks.

5 miles/1 hour and 25 minutes: christened "Pirates Cove" is an island dotted with sun-bleached driftwood pieces and narrow channels that allow paddling into the island's interior.

5.6 miles/1 hour and 40 minutes: 12' wide by 50' long island lies midstream; look to the right where railroad ties are embedded into the riverbank to create a sea wall. Behind the railroad ties a rolling hill featuring a broken stone wall draws your eyes to the home above.

5.7 miles/1 hour and 42 minutes: a long run of riffles take you past two midstream islands; ducks appear in large numbers. Once past the islands, the Northend Riverside Park take-out comes into view to the left.

5.9 miles/1 hour and 47 minutes: you are in! at the Northend Riverside Park take-out on the left bank. The park has restrooms, 3 pavilions, a sand volleyball court, and a kids' play area. The park is a favorite of Ferris State students for picnicking at the pavilions and launching tubing trips down the Muskegon from the park's river access. The White Pine Trail, for walking-hiking-biking, stretching from Cadillac in the north to Grand Rapids in the south, runs through the park and alongside the river.

Muskegon River Crack Research Team: Tom Holbrook, Yoshi Schlager, and Doc.

The College: Ferris State University

1201 S State St, Big Rapids MI 49307, ph 231-591-2000; www.ferris.edu

Born 1853 in a log cabin among the woods of Spencer, New York, was the founder of a private school that would become Ferris State, a future Michigan governor (elected in

1912 and 1914) and United States Senator (1922-1928), Woodbridge Nathan Ferris. In his youth, Ferris was a student at a public school, an experience that he later recalled as "the horror of his life". At age 18, he enrolled in the Oswego Normal (ie, teacher training) School at Oswego, New York, where Ferris was taught the "Pestalozzian" theory (authored by Johann Pestalozzi) of learning by doing rather than learning through theory, a major influence in Woodbridge Ferris' life. Upon his 1874 graduation from Oswego Normal School, Ferris became the principal of Spencer Free Academy, a position that confirmed his youthful negative view of public schools, prompting him to follow his dream of founding a private school. The dream was realized in 1884, when he moved his family to Big Rapids where Ferris opened a private institution, Big Rapids Industrial School, the forerunner of Ferris State University. In 1885, the Big Rapids Industrial School was renamed Ferris Industrial School, then Ferris Institute in 1898.

It is a bit of irony that, considering Woodbridge Ferris' distaste for public schools, Ferris State is the only public university in Michigan founded by an individual: on May 17, 1949, Governor G. Mennen Williams signed the bill making Ferris Institute a state college. The school was renamed Ferris State College in 1963 and then Ferris State University in 1987.

In 1928, 44 years after opening his private school, Woodbridge Nathan Ferris passed away in. The man popular enough to be elected both governor and senator was honored with a silent tribute by over 1,000 Ferris students and townsfolk who gathered at the Big Rapids train station under a drizzling rain as the funeral train pulled in. With Governor Fred W. Green in attendance, six military companies and the 126th infantry band marched in the funeral cortege to Highland View Cemetery in Big Rapids.

Up until 1930, sports teams representing the school were referred to as either "Spartans" or the "Ferrisites". That all changed during the 1930-1931 basketball season. The previous season had been the best in Ferris history and, with several returning key players, all were optimistic about 1930-1931. However, the basketball team was beset with an unusually high number of injuries, and player disqualifications due to rule changes, beginning the season by losing their first 5 games. Since teams then only played 18-game schedules, this was a huge hole to dig out from, but the men of Ferris did just that. Showing signs of a turnaround when the last of those 5 games lost were tough, 2-point losses, the team ended their losing streak in dramatic fashion by winning all remaining 13 games. Late in the season, a Big Rapids newspaper man asked Coach McElwain about the upcoming game versus an opponent known as the Bearcats, a game that appeared to be a particularly tough challenge. The newsman phrased the question to the coach this way, "what would happen if an irresistible force met an immovable object?" Coach McElwain said he believed the question might be solved when the "irresistible Central State Teachers College Bearcats met Ferris' immovable *Bulldogs*." Thankfully, the Ferris teams were never again referred to as "Ferrisites" and would be known as Bulldogs ever since.

At the 880-acre FSU main campus and its 19 off-campus sites across the state, 14,000 Bulldogs are enrolled in classes from associate to doctoral. More than 180 college degree programs are offered in Arts & Sciences, Business, Education and Human Services, Engineering Technology, Health Professions, Kendall College of Art and Design, Michigan College of Optometry, and Pharmacy.

Since 2006, 9 out of every 10 degrees offered at Ferris State align with what they define as an "in-demand occupation", more than any other university in Michigan. These are occupations in the categories of business, finance and management, administrative and clerical, computer science and engineering, social service, education and training, health care practitioners, health care technology and support, protective service, and construction, production and repair.

Somewhere, Bill Love is smiling.

The Tavern: Gypsy Nickel, 228 Baldwin Street, Big Rapids MI 49307; (231) 527-0085; www.gypsynickel.com.

The Gypsy Nickel can boast about one key point that no other bar can: they are located 80' from the Sawmill Canoe Livery. So, after you're done paddling the Muskegon with Sawmill, you don't need to move your vehicle to get to the post-paddling grub 'n grog 'cause you're already there.

Inside, the Gypsy Nickel isn't bad at all, with just the right amount of lighting (little) you'd want in a classic pub, a pool table, and a sweet, long bar you can belly up to... BUT, you want to go out the tavern door and on to their deck. The deck overlooks a gorgeous wide-water stretch of the Muskegon, with the sun sweetly glistening off the river's surface. If you need more sun than you soaked in while paddling, you got it here, but if you've had enough sunshine it's nice to know that most of the Gypsy's deck seats are in the shade.

The service was excellent, our waiter very accommodating, and the food overall rated pretty good/not great, but it did come quickly and, even if not the best, everything else about the Gypsy Tavern was just so great that we could live with food considered "pretty good".

The Gypsy offers 16 beers on tap, all of them craft beers, mostly Michigan brewed but from as far away as Australia's Foster Lager. But wait a minute, hold it right there!! Each Friday from 9PM to 1AM, the Gypsy Nickel sells $2 cans of Pabst Blue Ribbon beer, and $1.50 cans of Blatz, Black Label, and Hamm's! No wonder this tavern is so popular with Ferris State students: beer your Grandfather drank, from Milwaukee's finest to the Land of Sky Blue Water, at bargain prices. Oh yes sir, there will be a return trip to the Gypsy Nickel... so long as the old men can stay up for the 9PM specials start time.

Chapter Sources: Tom Holbrook, www.ferris.edu

Pine River / Alma College

Degree of Paddling Difficulty: beginner (level 1 of 3)

Livery: Ike's Mobile Kayak, (989) 750-5251, www.ikeskayaks.com; Ike's Mobile Kayak also services the Chippewa, the Tittabawassee, the Kawkawlin, and the Cedar rivers.

River Quote: "Watercraft was humankind's most important conveyance outside of walking" – Kirk Wipper

Pine River Soundtrack: In the Pines – Lead Belly, Boat on the River – Tommy Shaw, Take Five – Dave Brubeck, Many Rivers to Cross – Jimmy Cliff, Loch Lomond - Alma College Choir

Detroit Tigers radio station: listen to WQBX 104.9FM to follow the Tigers when paddling the Pine River near the Alma College campus.

Directions to the launch site: US127 to exit 124/St. Louis MI; Take Business 127 North (aka Main Street) into St. Louis; on Main Street, two blocks north of M46, is the Pine River on the south edge of Barnum River Park. Launch into the river at the NE corner of the Main Street Bridge, closest to the baseball park. Restrooms available.

Directions to the take-out: US127 to exit 124/St. Louis MI; Take Bus. 127 North (aka Main St.) into St. Louis, and turn right/east on M46. Follow M46 east for 2 miles to

Bagley Road and turn left/north. In 3 miles cross the river, access on left. Beyond the river, ask "Country Meadow Farms" (SW corner of Bagley & Riverside) for permission to park in their lot. No restrooms.

Background of the Pine River:

The Pine River near Alma College exceeded all expectations: the surprisingly fast river meandered gently through a thick forest with plenty of wildlife - it was wonderful! The Pine paddled for this chapter is not the river that first comes to mind when you suggest to friends "let's go canoe & kayak the Pine River in Michigan". *That* Pine River begins south of Cadillac in Tustin, runs west to a merger with the Manistee River near Wellston, and is one of the most frequently paddled rivers in the Midwest, known for its speed, rapids, and summer weekends crowded with canoes and kayaks. As great as that Pine is, *this* Pine River was one of the most pleasant surprises encountered in researching this book. The section of the Pine River outlined in this chapter, downstream of Alma College, takes paddlers on a peaceful and mostly shaded journey, as the current winds quietly through a shallow riverbed. It's a 5-mile long stretch, just downstream of the 103-mile long river's midpoint. This Pine's headwaters rise in Mecosta County. From there, the water flows southeast for almost 50 miles to the village of Sumner, where the river pivots to the northeast, meandering through Alma and St. Louis, until its confluence with the Chippewa River, two miles west of where the Chippewa merges with the Tittabawassee River beneath the 3-legged bridge known as "the Tridge" in Midland. Fishermen encountered on the paddle had been catching carp and smallmouth bass.

Acting as good stewards of the river is the group Friends of the Pine. Members include private residents and folks from Alma College, local government, and non-profits. The

Friends' stated objective is to "Work to protect the watershed, improve water quality and wildlife habitat, to limit erosion and to support recreational use of the Pine River". Among their efforts have been river clean-ups and development of access points and river maps. For information on Friends of the Pine, call 989-875-5278. The Friends had no website when this book went to publication.

Camping: Located 7 miles southwest of Alma, near where the Pine flow turns from southeast to northeast, is the Leisure Lake Campground. Spread along the banks of a 35-acre lake, the LLC offers 140 campsites, water & electric hookups, 3 rental cabins, 2 pavilions, showers, firewood delivered to the sites, and a camp store.

The Leisure Lake Campground is located at 505 S. Warner Road, Sumner MI 48889; phone 989-875-4689; www.leisurelakefamilycampground.com

Paddling the Pine River:

- Total trip 5.2 miles, 1 hour and 30 minutes (contact the livery for Pine trip options)

The Main Street access is downstream and within sight of the St. Louis dam at Barnum River Park. As you launch, the river is 60' wide and 2' deep, about what you will find most of the paddle (as narrow as 30', depths from 1' to 3'). The June trip water level was considered "normal". The river floor is sandy, sprinkled with occasional big rocks up to 3' in length that require your attention.

Two minutes from the launch, you encounter a short rapids run below the footbridge, a rare whitewater sighting on this stretch of the Pine.

1 mile/16 minutes: a mini-waterfall is created by water cascading into the river from a tunnel on the left. 3 blue herons soar above within the first river mile.

1.3 miles/22 minutes: left bank home with a 2nd floor balcony sits on an undulating hillside, a very pretty setting. Two deer drink along the right bank.

1.7 miles/28 minutes: a cantilevered deck over the right bank precedes by 4 minutes the universally agreed upon ideal party house a few hundred feet beyond the right shore.

2.1 miles/35 minutes: pass below the McGregor Road bridge; downstream, at the end of a long straightaway, a home sits on a left bluff as the Pine bends right, offering its tenants a spectacular river view.

Riverside Drive runs beyond the left bank for most of today's paddle, visible in small doses. The Riverside Drive homes are, for the most part, modest – nice to see affordable housing with such an outstanding view of this pretty river.

2.4 miles/40 minutes: tiny creek merges from the left near land well-used by the homeowner for riverside relaxing. The beauty of the Pine and the thick forest that surrounds it, along with the plentiful wildlife, is a visual delight.

3 miles/50 minutes: at the straightaway's end and above the tree line rises a wind turbine.

3.6 miles/1 hour: paddle beneath the twin power lines.

4 miles/1 hour and 7 minutes: very big & very close to shore lurks a hulking red barn.

4.6 miles/1 hour and 18 minutes: pass alongside an island to the left of midstream. 5 minutes downstream paddle below telephone lines. A family of ducks swims along the left bank.

5.2 miles/1 hour and 30 minutes: you're in! on the left and just before the Bagley Road Bridge.

Pine River Crack Research Team: Glenn Isenhart, Steve Arnosky, JJ Johnson, Doc.

The College: Alma College

614 W. Superior Street, Alma MI 48801, 989-463-7111; www.alma.edu

Quarterbacking the Alma College football team in 1957-1959 while earning recognition as a Small College All-American, was a native of nearby St. Louis, Michigan, an athletic standout also in basketball, baseball and track, future Detroit Tiger Jim Northrup. Yes, the man also known in his days with the Tigers as the Gray Fox aka the Silver Fox, the man who to this day holds the Major League Baseball record of 3 grand slam home runs in 1 week, the man who tripled in the winning run over Curt Flood's head in the deciding game 7 of the 1968 World Series, yes THAT Jim Northrup was a star athlete with the Alma Scots. As the team quarterback, he was 3rd in the entire USA in total offense in 1959 (1,538 yards). Although he would be an outfielder with the Tigers, for the Scots baseball team he pitched a no-hitter against Calvin in 1958. For the Scots track team, Northrup set the college broad jump record and held it for several years. After graduating from Alma, Jim signed with the Tigers in the spring of 1960. The National Football League wanted him, but as Northrup said, "I was born to play baseball".

"Nobody loves the sound of bagpipes more than Alma College Scots" says the Alma College website and, once exposed to the campus, you will be a believer. The "Scotland, USA" sign welcoming folks to the Alma city limits ensures that there will be no surprises. Alma College attracts students from all across the country to their Highland Arts programs (dancing, piping, fiddling, and drumming), considered by many to be among the finest in the land, learning from instructors who are USA and world champions in their specialty. The Alma College Pipe Band performs seemingly non-stop, from the students welcoming convocation to commencement ceremony. It's a plaid, plaid world at Alma: the marching band performs every football game in their kilts/the Kiltie Dancers bring sunshine on a cloudy day with their grace and rhythm/ there is even a *Scottish Pride* flavor ice cream (including Lorna Doone cookies, of course, and chocolate ice cream) served at the College Corner Coffee and Books store.

Each year the Alma College campus is home to the Alma Highland Festival. The caber toss alone is worth your attendance - there is something particularly intriguing in watching men in kilts throwing telephone poles great distances ("wear kilts and caber on" the participants t-shirts read). Other athletic events include the sheaves tossing (a sheaf is a bundle of straw wrapped in a burlap bag and tossed with a pitchfork over a raised bar – feels strange just typing this), stone toss (similar to shot put) and the hammer toss. Competition in dancing, piping, and fiddling, musical entertainment, reenactment camp and clan gathering, arts and crafts, Scottish food and vendors, a beverage and entertainment tent, and, yes, you may bring your dog. For more information, go to www.almahighlandfestival.com.

The 128-acre Alma College campus, in addition to a 200-acre ecological tract, is home to 1,400 undergraduate students. The college awards five degrees: Bachelor of Arts, Bachelor of Science, Bachelor of Science in Nursing, Bachelor of Fine Arts, & Bachelor of Music. Programs producing the most grads are Biology, Business Administration, Education, English, Highland Arts, History, Integrative Physiology and Health Science, and Psychology.

Alma College has been ranked among the "Best in the Midwest" by The Princeton's Review and has received high marks from the Fiske Guide to Colleges. Colleges of Distinction, a national college guide for students, identified Alma College as "one of the best places to learn, grow and succeed".

Plaid works!

The Tavern: Bravehearts Pub, 218 E. Superior St., Alma MI 48801; (989) 466-2309; www.braveheartspub.com

You're greeted by a couple of make-you-smile attention getters when you walk in the front door at Bravehearts... "Nothing says let's celebrate America quite like drinking beer and playing with explosives" the sign posted at the end of the bar tells you, and nearby is a photo of a very happy 1950s moment as Gordie Howe, Ted Lindsey, and Alex Delvecchio are smoking Stanley Cup victory cigars.

Bravehearts Pub is located in a late-1800s building along the main road which runs through both the Alma College campus and downtown Alma. The Pub has a nice old-time back bar framed by the structure's original brick wall, and the ceiling is the style of tin so popular in the 1880s/90s. Its "Bravehearts" name and a bit 'o the décor fits in nicely with the town's self-proclaimed status as "Scotland, USA".

Pabst on tap! Pabst on tap! is the lead beer of the 16 beers on tap offered by Bravehearts. You will need some of that brewed and fermented beverage to wash down the "Great Scot", two half-pound patties topped with bacon. During the Tuesday visit, the daily special was a $5 make your own salad. The menu includes wraps, sandwiches, burgers, appetizers, quesadillas, nachos and salads – all at prices within reach of the local college students.

Bravehearts has two pool tables, two dart boards, nice juke box, 6 big screen TVs, and covers its walls with a good amount of Detroit Tigers photos and references. The building was a meat market as recently as the 1960s (not a pick up joint, but an actual meat market), and the scars where the meat hooks once hung are slightly visible in the ceiling. The meat market was transformed into a pub, then another pub, then Bravehearts in 1999.

Papa Herbert Roy Fletcher would've loved the sign, "No Shoes, No Kilt, No Service". What a fine way to say good-bye to Bravehearts Pub.

Chapter Sources: Steve Arnosky, Wikipedia, www.alma.edu

Red Cedar River / Michigan State University

Degree of Paddling Difficulty: intermediate (level 2 of 3); only skilled paddlers should paddle through the rapids at the MSU Administration Building (3.7 miles into the trip)

Livery: River Town Adventures, 325 City Market Dr., Lansing MI 48912, (517) 253-7523; owners Nate Williams & Paul Brogan also service the Grand River; www.rivertownadventures.com

River Quote: "At what point does a flotilla become an armada?" - Allen Deming

Red Cedar River Soundtrack: Over the Red Cedar – Charlie Parr, Steamboat Queen – Steppin' In It, Amazing Journey – the Who, A Pirate Looks at 40 – Jimmy Buffett, Victory for MSU – MSU Marching Band

Detroit Tigers radio affiliate: listen to WJIM 1240AM to follow the Tigers when paddling the Red Cedar near the Michigan State University campus.

Directions to the launch site: I-96 to exit 110/Okemos Road (first exit east of Lansing), north on Okemos Road past Mt. Hope Road to Ferguson Park, located just before (south of) the bridge over the Red Cedar. Turn right into Ferguson Park. Restrooms available.

Directions to the take-out: US127 to exit 77/Kalamazoo St. exit in Lansing; west on Kalamazoo St. past Dagwood's Tavern to Clemens Avenue and turn left (south). Continue south on Clemens as it becomes Aurelius Road and, after crossing over the Red Cedar River, turn left (east) into Ralph W. Crego Park. The Kruger's Landing launch is inside Crego Park. Restrooms available.

- Pizza tip bonus: we found that bringing a couple of Bell's pizzas to the launch site stops hunger, wins friends, creates happiness, and makes a day on the river even better than you thought possible. Pre-paddling, make the pick-up at Bell's Greek Pizza on 1135 E. Grand River Ave, East Lansing, (517) 332-0858.

Background of the Red Cedar River:

The Red Cedar River runs from east to west for 45 miles until it empties into the Grand River in Lansing. Its headwaters flow out of Cedar Lake, south of Fowlerville. From there, the river winds its way through Williamston, Okemos, East Lansing, and into Lansing. Pike and steelhead swim its waters. This is a river blessed with many excellent stewards...

- The host livery, River Town Adventures, holds 4 Red Cedar River cleanups each year, providing free boats for the day to MSU students who volunteer to assist with the effort (an average of 30 students volunteer per event). Info at www. rivertownadventures.com.

- The MSU Fisheries and Wildlife Club, along with the MSU Scuba Club, conducts a river cleanup each semester, with some picking up trash from a canoe and others scuba diving for trash from the river floor. Their past efforts have removed from the river bicycles, street signs, trash bins, tires and parking meters – all sent to the campus Surplus Store and Recycling Center, making the cleanup a zero-waste event. The Fisheries and Wildlife Club website is www. msufwclub.weebly.com.

- The MSU Institute of Water Research and the MSU Landscape Services have created riverside vegetative buffers that filter out pollutants from the river.

- Each October LOAPC, aka the Lansing Oar and Paddle Club, organizes the "Red Cedar River Clean and Clear Project", encouraging volunteers to come on out with their waders, wetsuits, and chain saws. To learn more about the clean-up and about the various LOAPC social paddle outings, go to their website at www. loapc.wordpress.com.

Camping: The Lansing Cottonwood Campground has been field tested and highly rated by crack researchers Lindsay and Don Rogers, and is located just a few feet from the end of the trip outlined in this chapter. The LCC offers 145 total camp sites, ranging from rustic (no hook-ups) to full hook-up (water, electric, and sewer), and their amenities include laundry, hot showers, camp store, lobby and rec room, pool, playground, horseshoe pits, a volleyball court, softball fields, and a football/soccer field. The LCC property has 2 ponds with kayaks and paddleboats. Their address is 5339 Aurelius Road (just south of the river), Lansing MI 48911, 517-393-3200; www.lansingcottonwoodcampground.com.

Paddling the Red Cedar River:

- Total trip 7 miles, 3 hours & 20 minutes (see livery website for 2 other Red Cedar trips)

Launching at Ferguson Park, you're embarking on the trip that River Town Adventures refers to as "Spartan Nation", taking you through the heart of the Michigan State

University campus. The paddle for this book took place in April, when water levels were slightly higher than "normal" summer time conditions. At the launch, the river is 2' deep, 60' wide, and in a few feet you're beneath the Okemos Road Bridge.

Note: during much higher water on a previous early-May trip, the result of 3" of rainfall the day before, the flooded river rocketed us downstream for 10.6 miles at 3 hours & 15 minutes, much faster than the 3 hours & 20 minutes required to paddle today's 7 miles. Kruger Landing was the same end for both trips (early-May trip started at Legg Park on Van Atta Road in Okemos). The higher water of the previous early-May paddle made the rapids at the MSU Administration Building more treacherous than they were today.

.8 mi/29 minutes: at the big right bend are the first homes on today's journey, visible behind a concrete sea wall on the left bank.

1 mile/37 minutes: Indian Hills Golf Course plays beyond the riverbank to the left as you paddle beneath Nakoma Drive Bridge. You'll pass by the golf course clubhouse in 3 minutes.

1.4 miles/49 minutes: the Red Cedar widens into a small lake/large pond with an island on the far right. The most direct outlet from the lake is in the distance to the left, a 5-minute paddle. As the lake narrows back into the river, there is a man-made stone dam that may be easily floated over in high water or may obstruct your paddle in low water. To avoid this dam, when you first enter the small lake/large pond, take the longer route right and around the island, allowing you to reconnect with the main body of the river several feet downstream of the dam.

A fisherman at the river's edge tells us he pulled in 5 pike from the Red Cedar yesterday. Deer, turtles and ducks dot the river and its banks while birds warble a melodic surround sound. Nice!

1.8 miles/1 hour and 5 minutes: pass below a railroad bridge.

2.3 miles/1 hour and 20 minutes: beyond the left bank stands Hubbard Hall, once the largest dorm for a public university in the world, and the first piece of MSU property you pass by today.

2.7 miles/1 hour and 28 minutes: a nesting goose on the left shore tries to ignore the flotilla, a few feet before the Hagadorn Road Bridge crosses the Red Cedar. The Lansing River Trail, a popular biking, hiking, and running trail, now runs parallel to the river along the left shore. The LRT will cross the river twice during today's paddle and, from Hagadorn Road to the west, runs alongside the Red Cedar to the trip's take-out.

3.2 miles/1 hour and 43 minutes: paddle beneath the Bogue Street Bridge. Past the bridge and along the shore are golden forsythias and to the right is the Kresge Art Center. 6 students have been seen lying or swinging in hammocks along the shoreline. Robert Shaw Hall is on the left and the Farm Lane Bridge is visible in the distance.

3.4 miles/1 hour and 49 minutes: MSU Auditorium is on the right. Crack researcher Allen Deming recalls attending rock concerts here in the 70s, but the crowds were too rowdy and these shows were moved to Jenison Fieldhouse (where rock-and-roll-wild was more easily tolerated). MSU Dairy, in Allen Deming's opinion the finest ice cream in the world, is available at Anthony Hall (to your left & just before the Farm Lane Road Bridge) and at the student union.

3.5 miles/1 hour and 52 minutes: "The Rock", famous MSU landmark and a gift of the class of 1873, sits on the right shore, visible just before passing below Farm Lane Road.

3.7 miles/2 hours: you've reached the **Red Cedar Rapids** with the MSU Administration Building on the right. Running these rapids is for experienced paddlers only – all others should portage (in late-summer, the river may be so low that you have to walk the boats though this stretch). Several boats in our flotilla portaged these rapids, taking out on the right bank and putting-in just downstream of the rapids' whitewater (in higher water it is easy to portage at the concrete steps on the left bank), while 6 kayaks and canoes ran the rapids (all excitedly and safely). There was much scrapping of the boats against the rocks in the rapids, leading to today's term "schoo-ching" the rapids. Watching paddlers run these rapids is quite the Michigan State University spectator sport, stopping riverside walkers in their tracks and turning them into photographers.

4 miles/ 2 hours and 7 minutes: Spartan Stadium, home of the football team since 1923, towers over the trees on the left. To the right, the W.J Beal Botanical Gardens, the oldest continuously-operated university botanical gardens in the USA (created by MSU Professor William James Beal in 1873). The Beaumont Tower and its carillon with 49 bells (the symbol of Michigan State per crack researcher Don Rogers) peals beyond the botanical gardens.

Passing beneath Kalamazoo Street, the Sparty statue stands proudly on the left. The sounds of nature are all around: the sweet singing of birds, the peaceful yawning of paddlers, and the ping of an aluminum bat meeting a baseball as the MSU baseball team practices at Drayton McLane Baseball Stadium to the left, just downstream from Sparty.

4.5 miles/2 hours and 21 minutes: there is a sweet little rapids run as the river bends left, preceding the first view of the Kellogg Center on the right shore. Jenison Fieldhouse is to the left followed by the Breslin Center.

4.8 miles/2 hours and 28 minutes: paddle beneath the Harrison Road Bridge with the Brody complex on the right. The drain embedded in the left bank, along with its concrete remnants, once drained the old fish hatchery.

5.6 miles/2 hours and 52 minutes: Dagwood's Tavern is a 5-minute walk west when passing under today's 2nd Kalamazoo Road Bridge. 5 minutes downstream, the dirt right bank may be used as a river access, with a parking lot just beyond.

5.9 miles/3 hours: pass below US127.

6.1 miles/3 hours and 2 minutes: pass below I-496. The Lansing Sewage Treatment Center processes on the left just past 496. A railroad trestle will cross over the river in 4 minutes.

6.4 miles/3 hours and 8 minutes: the Lansing River Trail crosses overhead.

7 miles/3 hours and 20 minutes: after passing a creek merging from the left and paddling alongside the Lansing River Trail, you are in! at the Kruger Landing boat ramp in Ralph W. Crego Park on the left.

Red Cedar Crack Research Team: Allen Deming, Nate Williams, Paul Brogan, Yasu Miura, Lori Breslin, Lindsay Rogers, Don Rogers, Ande Rogers, Katy Fritts, John Steck, Sue Thompson, Maddie Craig, Chris Weaks, David Green, James Green, Rachel Ewald, Alex Pereida, Trent Bekker, Alex Diaz, Maggie and Doc

The College: Michigan State University

220 Trowbridge Road, East Lansing MI 48824, phone 517-355-1855; www.msu.edu.

On the banks of the Red Cedar... the Sparty Statue, dedicated on June 9, 1945, 9' 7" tall, weighing in at 6,600 pounds, and the largest free-standing bronze structure in the world.

"The campus of the college was only a clearing in the great Michigan forest" was a local observation when the *Agricultural College of the State of Michigan* was founded in 1855. One-half century before the area was called East Lansing, what was taking shape around Michigan Avenue and its junction with Harrison Road was known as "Collegetown", authorized by the Michigan legislature as a college for teaching scientific agriculture – the first such university in the United States. The institute's goal was to make scientists of farmers, the state's largest occupational group in the mid-1850s,

153

by teaching them proven techniques of how to get the most out of their land. Once educated at this new Agricultural College, graduates would return to their home farm where they would apply what they learned. Neighbors would watch and absorb this new wisdom, as would their neighbors, and their neighbors, as the knowledge would radiate out or *extend out*, improving production throughout Michigan and beyond. To extend out this wisdom was Theodore Roosevelt's theme as he gave the 1907 commencement speech at (what was then known as) the State Agricultural College. TR asked that "land grant" colleges such as MSU be "at the forefront of *extending* to Michigan residents new farming and homemaking techniques to improve everyday living". Today, the Michigan State University "Extension Services" fans out its knowledge and resources throughout the state, enhancing standards of living in all walks of life.

The early MSU had been known as a "land grant college" for over 40 years before President Roosevelt's 1907 campus speech...

The "Land Grant Act" aka the Morrill Act, was signed into law by President Abraham Lincoln in 1862. The law rewarded colleges that "educated the industrial (working) classes in several pursuits and professions in life", allowing the average folk to obtain a practical education in agriculture, engineering, and military tactics. The State Agricultural College, the prototype college for the Morrill Act, received from the federal government an 1860s land grant of a quarter million acres in the northern Lower Peninsula (sold off later by MSU to create a $1M endowment). Eventually these land grants were replaced by yearly $50,000 appropriations to each eligible college. Two land grant schools, MSU and Penn State, annually compete in football for the Land Grant Trophy.

Michigan State University has gone through 6 name changes: from its February 12, 1855 inception as the Agricultural College of the State of Michigan to 1861 State Agricultural College to 1909 Michigan Agricultural College to 1925 Michigan State College of Agriculture and Applied Science to 1955 Michigan State University of Agriculture and Applied Science to January 1, 1964 Michigan State University.

Huge and sprawling defines Michigan State University: 5,200 campus acres, with an additional 2,100 acres in existing or planned development, and 538 buildings. As of 2015, the student enrollment is 50,085, representing all 83 Michigan counties, all 50 USA states, plus another 130 countries. Beyond East Lansing are 19,600 Michigan acres used for agricultural and natural resources extension services. MSU offers more than 200 programs of undergraduate, graduate, and professional study with degree-granting colleges of Agriculture and Natural Resources, Arts and Humanities, Arts and Letters, Business, Communication Arts and Sciences, Education, Engineering, Human Medicine, Law, Music, Natural Science, Nursing, Osteopathic Medicine, Social Science, and Veterinary Medicine.

MSU recognition and ranking...

- First institution of higher learning in the United States to teach scientific agriculture.

- More than 275 study abroad programs on all continents in more than 60 countries.

- Ranks in top 10 for both study abroad participation and international student enrollment.

- Selected by the U.S. Department of Energy to design and establish the Facility for Rare Isotope Beams, a $730 million facility that will advance understanding of rare nuclear isotopes and the evolution of the cosmos.

- Ranks sixth among large universities for producing Peace Corps volunteers with 2,322 alumni serving since 1961.

- Tom Izzo, Mark Dantonio, and Magic Johnson.

- Reaches into all 83 counties in Michigan through MSU Extension to share resources with individuals, communities, and businesses.

- *U.S. News & World Report* ranks MSU 75th among the world's top 100 universities and 35th among the nation's public universities.

- First in the nation for 20 straight years for graduate programs in elementary and secondary education.

- First in the nation for graduate programs in nuclear physics and industrial and organizational psychology.

- First in the nation for undergraduate program in supply chain.

- Ranks 82nd among 400 global universities in the 2014-15 World University Rankings by *Times Higher Education*.

- Silver rating from the Association for the Advancement of Sustainability in Higher Education's STARS program, which measures and encourages sustainability in education and research, operations, and planning, administration, and engagement.

- Only university in the country with on-campus medical schools graduating allopathic (MD) and osteopathic (DO) physicians, and veterinarians (DVMs).

- MSU's outstanding National Public Radio station WKAR, 90.5FM, features NPR national programs, local classical music programming and the excellent "Current State" morning show that covers news and issues of the day with long-time host Mark Bashore.

- Bell's Greek Pizza at 1135 E. Grand River Ave in East Lansing, (517) 332-0858, cannot be mentioned too many times.

The Tavern #1: Crunchy's, 254 W. Grand River Avenue, East Lansing MI 48823; (517) 351-2506; www.crunchyseastlanding.com

Getting MSU students, family and friends stuffed and half-in-the-wrapper since 1982, Crunchy's was opened by Paul "Crunchy" Grattarola on October 18 of that year – possibly in honor of the 206th anniversary of the first "cock tail" ever served (October 18, 1776 in a New York tavern decorated with a bird's tail). The bar is a 5-minute walk north of where the Red Cedar River winds its way around MSU's Drayton McLane's Baseball Stadium (the 4 mile mark of the 7 mile trip detailed in this chapter).

The table's waitress' name was Nona, the Italian word for Grandmother. Unfortunately, this Nona did not bring ravioli or risotto to our table but, being Sunday at Crunchy's, Nona the waitress did bring half-price pizza, arriving with generous quantities of spices baked in, and a very nice flavor to it.

Our post-paddling arrival by 530PM just beat the rush: astonishingly for a Sunday, a long line had formed by 7PM to get into the tavern. Crunchy's is a packed, loud, fun environment. Beer may be purchased by the glass or by the bucket (strangely, if sitting in the outdoor patio, you may not buy a bucket of beer but glass is ok). By the bucket is how you can also buy fries (not bad), onion rings (not great), sliders (a lot of bread), and tots – now we've hit the jackpot. One of our tables ordered a bucket of tots and liked 'em so much that each and every person at that table also ordered tots as their side dish to go with their meals.

The MSU alum in our group were life-long fans of the Crunchy burgers, among other reasons citing the fact that the highly-regarded MSU Dairy Store provides all Crunchy's sliced cheddar and jalapeno jack cheese. The half-pound, char-grilled, Crunchy burger has made Yahoo's annual list of the "21 Best College Burgers in America".

27 craft beers are available, along with such standards as Dos Equis, Corona, Labatt's, and Leinenkugel. Bringing out your beer order in 24 ounce glasses is the default unless you say otherwise. We were all impressed by the amount of 24 ounce glasses of beer Nona could carry at once – the tip Maggie offered was informing Nona this would lead to arthritis eventually.

- Pizza tip bonus #2: Sitting outside at Crunchy's, right across the street is Goomba's Pizza, employer of Crack Researcher Alex Diaz. Many paddlers had high praise for Goomba's. Something about their Pokey Stix...

Crunchy's was overall a fine place to relive the magic of the Red Cedar over their grub 'n grog. If you decide differently, you can always have Goomba's run a pie over to you.

The Tavern #2: the Harrison Roadhouse, 720 Michigan Avenue, East Lansing MI 48823; (517) 337-0200; www.harrisonroadhouse.com

Based in personal experience, do not shout out anything positive about the University of Michigan while standing or sitting or existing inside of the Harrison Roadhouse.

Even if you are wearing a Spartans sweatshirt, the Roadhouse staff does not want to hear about how folks living in the state should all pull for each other. This is probably basic knowledge for most, but some of us are still naïve.

Any such personal experience does not stop me from shouting hosannas about what a fun place the Harrison Roadhouse is, especially during football season. Bellied up to the bar (and what a back bar it is!), or at tables near the bar, or out on the patio are all enjoyable places to be. The crack research team has spent an unusually large amount of time in confirming that the Harrison Roadhouse is worthy of a good review. The wait staff is personable, patient, and on top of things. The food has long earned two thumbs up, whether we order sandwiches, starters, burgers, wraps, or full meals. On tap are over 20 beers, heavy on craft beers plus the old time goodness of Labatt's and, for those watching their girlish figures, Miller Lite and Bud Light.

The Roadhouse is a 2-minute walk from the north bank of the Red Cedar, near the Kellogg Center. *Go Green, Go White, Go Canoeing...*

Wait! The chapter is not over yet! If, after filling yourself up post-paddle at Bell's or Crunchy's, or the Harrison Roadhouse, or any other fine East Lansing/Lansing establishment, you find that it's one of those nights that shouts for ice cream... head 10 miles east to Williamston and visit the "Twister" at 204 E. Grand River. Maggie knows her flurries, has enjoyed many at a wide variety of ice cream shops, and her favorite is the Hawaiian Flurry at the Twister.

Chapter Sources: Paul Brogan, Nate Williams, Allen Deming, Don Rogers, "At the Campus Gates" by Kestenbaum-Kuhn-Anderson-Green, www.msu.edu

Rouge River / UM Dearborn

Degree of Paddling Difficulty: intermediate (level 2 of 3)

Livery: Heavner Canoe & Kayak Rental, 2775 Garden Road, Milford MI 48381, (248) 685-2379; www.heavercanoe.com

River Quote: "What better place is there to hone communication skills than in a canoe?" – Al Heavner

Rouge River Soundtrack: River of Dreams – Glenn Frey, Ferry Me – the Normandies, Lord Mister Ford – Jerry Reed, Just Fine – Shotgun Soul, Dancing on the Water – Bob James

Detroit Tigers radio stations: listen to WXYT 1270AM or 97.1FM to follow the Tigers when paddling the Rouge near the UM Dearborn campus.

Directions to the launch site: US24 to Michigan Ave., east on Michigan to downtown Dearborn, turn north/left on Monroe Street, take Monroe St. to Ford Field access. Restrooms available.

Directions to the take-out: I-94 to Oakwood exit/206, Oakwood southeast/right to Allen Road, northeast/left on Allen to Dearborn Road (street before Greenfield) and turn northwest/ left. The Melvindale Community Event Center will be on your right. Restrooms available.

- Classic burger bonus: Carter's Hamburgers is at Outer Drive & Southfield, between the launch and take-out sites (think Bates/Top Hat/Green's/Bray's burgers)

Background of the Rouge River:

The 4 branches of the Rouge River flow for 126 miles through Wayne, Washtenaw and Oakland counties. The Main branch meanders south from its headwaters in Rochester Hills. On its way to a rendezvous with the Detroit River, it absorbs first the Upper Rouge in Livonia, then the Middle branch in Dearborn Heights, and finally the Lower branch in Dearborn. After merging with the Lower branch, the Main turns to the southwest as it passes through Melvindale and Detroit on its way to a confluence with the Detroit River.

The two branches paddled for this chapter are the Lower and the Main. At their merger is fascination past, present, and future. Past: Henry Ford, Thomas Edison, Harvey Firestone, and John Burroughs (aka the 4 Vagabonds) conversing in chairs along the riverbank at Ford's Fair Lane Estate. Present: stunning view as you paddle by the Fair Lane home, waterfall, and dam. Future: a cooperative effort to expand recreational use in and along the Rouge by the city of Dearborn and Greenfield Village. Plans are in various stages to develop along Dearborn's riverbanks historical signage and public access points - including an access at Greenfield Village's Oxbow Park that would open up Rouge canoeing and kayaking to Village visitors.

Alongside UM-Dearborn and the Henry Ford Estate are the offices of the outstanding steward of the Rouge River and its watershed, the Friends of the Rouge. Since forming in 1986, FOTR organizes annual "Rouge Rescue" cleanups in communities along the river, motivating local residents, businesses, and government agencies to work together in restoring its health. The use of the Rouge as a sewer and as a place to dispose of industrial waste has been minimized, invasive species and tons of trash removed from its waters, and native plants installed. The health of the Rouge is reflected in local fishermen's stories of catching salmon, carp, catfish, trout, bluegill, northern pike, perch, smallmouth and largemouth bass. The river restoration improves wildlife viewing: on this Rouge paddle were sighted kingfishers, beavers, cormorants, blue herons, turtles & sandpipers - plus a mink that ran on the bank next to our canoe for 50'. To follow the on-going efforts of the Friends of the Rouge, a blessing to all who love Michigan, go to www.therouge.org.

A special thanks for their yeoman efforts ensuring a paddling path was open for this chapter's trip goes to Jeff Vallender, Eric Long, Bill Craig and the Friends of the Rouge.

Paddling the Rouge River:

- Total trip 4.9 miles, 2 hours & 5 minutes (check Rouge paddling options with the livery or the Friends of the Rouge websites, both listed earlier in this chapter)

The Ford Field access is to the left of the quaint covered bridge. Enter on a gentle dirt slope into the bay. Paddle across the bay 75' to a right turn into the Lower Branch of the Rouge. Once in the river, paddle beneath the Ford Field covered bridge and a 2nd pedestrian bridge within the first 5 minutes of the trip, enjoying nice rapids runs at both bridges.

.4 mile/10 minutes: paddle beneath the Brady Street Bridge. Depth has varied between 2' to 4' with a width of 30'.

.6 mile/16 minutes: at left bend, a cool looking concrete & brick storm drain extends from the right shore where Morley Street comes to an end. Kingfishers and the first of many Cormorants have been spotted (at one point today, 12 Cormorants were seen in a single tree!).

.8 mile/20 minutes: Andiamo's Restaurant (formerly Chicago Roadhouse) is visible upon the hill to the right, at what was once Thompson's Landing (off Brady, one-half block north of Michigan Avenue), a location for loading/unloading armaments during the Civil War. The landing and the abandoned building alongside the river's right served as the Powder Magazine for the Detroit Arsenal in old Dearbornville beginning in the 1830s. By the 1950s, Dearborn's Historical Society was located in this structure.

The river now runs south of Andiamo's Restaurant but it used to flow beneath it until MDOT widened Michigan Avenue, changing the river's course. The structure housing Andiamo's is built on 100' deep caissons as the soil is too poor to support it.

1.3 miles/38 minutes: the river bends left with Michigan Avenue traffic on the right. The Lower Rouge soon turns away from Michigan Avenue and is now at its most attractive, widening to 40' and flowing under a beautiful canopy of trees leaning in from the banks.

1.5 miles/43 minutes: a fantastic sight greets you as the Lower Rouge you've been paddling empties into the Main Rouge (the Main flows towards you from the left) - look left/upstream on the Main: 1/10th of a mile away is Fair Lane, the Henry Ford Estate, its dam, and waterfall in all of its bygone splendor. The view is spectacular as you paddle towards the Ford Estate.

1.6 miles/47 minutes: reach the foot of the waterfall. The building to the right with the gorgeous chimney is the dam's powerhouse, with two stone tunnels beneath it. To the left of the powerhouse is the dam and waterfall, both in front of the Henry Ford Estate where Ford spent his last moments. Turn and paddle back towards the Lower Rouge.

1.7 miles/54 minutes: paddling the Main, you pass by the Lower branch merging from the right. Absorbing the volume of the Lower Rouge, the Main Rouge widens to 70'. Bicyclers cross above on the pedestrian bridge that is a few feet downstream of the merger. To your left or east, the riverbanks and beyond are property of the University of Michigan-Dearborn.

2 miles/1 hour: paddle below the Evergreen Road Bridge. An amazingly large number of turtles are viewed, as many as 14 on a log.

2.2 miles/1 hour and 6 minutes: pass under Michigan Avenue, with the Fair Lane Town Center on the left. At this point, the Rouge flows over a concrete river floor, created to minimize flooding. Greenfield Village is now on your right.

2.5 miles/1 hour and 11 minutes: if you are in the mood to explore, turn right off the Main branch and paddle the channel beneath the pedestrian bridge into Greenfield

Village's Oxbow Park (possibly, the site of a future canoe/kayak access). The park's natural riverbed replaces the river's concrete floor, and it is home to dozens of Blue Herons, Sandpipers, and Cormorants.

2.8 miles/1 hour and 20 minutes: wrap up the side exploration, departing Oxbow Park to return to the Main Branch of the Rouge. Follow the Main's current as it flows to the right.

3 miles/1 hour and 23 minutes: pass under the Southfield Freeway.

3.4 miles/1 hour and 34 minutes: Detroit Water and Sewer is beyond the left bank. The river runs very straight in its concrete basin with Rotunda Drive clearly visible downstream.

3.9 miles/1 hour and 43 minutes: paddle beneath Rotunda Drive. You will immediately see on the right a large gray building, the Detroit Lions Allen Park training facility. Although Allen Park claims it, 82% of the structure sits within the Dearborn city limits.

4.6 miles/2 hours: pass under the I-94 expressway.

4.9 miles/2 hours and 5 minutes: you're in! on the right bank at the Melvindale Community Events Center.

Rouge Crack Research Team: Dave Norwood, Alan Heavner, Chris Wall, Ameera Chaaban, Jeff Vallender, Eric Long, Bill Craig, Sally Petrella, Paul Stark, Erin Cassady, Sue Thompson, Paul Draus, Terry Bakewell, Lisa Perez, Vicki Schroeder, Bill Dunphy, Chris Weaks, MagDoc.

The College: University of Michigan-Dearborn

4901 Evergreen Road, Dearborn MI 48128, phone 313-593-5000; www.umdearborn.edu

In 1909, the Detroit Tigers & Ty Cobb lost the World Series to the Pittsburgh Pirates & Honus Wagner. That year, Tiger fan Henry Ford assuaged his sadness over the Series outcome by purchasing a 200-acre farm from a neighboring family, property Ford tilled while conducting a variety of tractor experiments (Fordson tractors were built at the Ford River Rouge Complex before an auto was ever produced there). In 1956, the land was donated to the University of Michigan for the purpose of creating a university extension campus. 3 years later that university extension opened under the name of UM-Dearborn Center, renamed UM Dearborn Campus in 1963. The 1970s opened with the school renamed in 1971 as the University of Michigan-Dearborn and concluded with a 10-year enrollment growth from 1,000 to 6,000 by 1979.

Today, the student population has grown to almost 10,000 on the 200-acre campus, with 70 of those acres maintained as a nature reserve along the Rouge River. The University of Michigan-Dearborn has long been known for outstanding management and engineering programs, with the College of Computer Science & Engineering and the College of Business considered among the best nationally. UMD offers over 90 academic majors, 28 masters degree programs, and 3 doctoral degree programs.

UMD's national recognition includes...

- US News & World Report has ranked UMD 6th among master-level universities in the United States.

- The Princeton Review has listed the College of Business among the country's best every year since 2008.

- The Corporation for National and Community Service named UMD to the President's Higher Education Community Service Honor Roll, the highest federal recognition a college or university can receive for commitment to volunteering.

There have been some impressive visitors to the UM-Dearborn campus, including 3 Presidents: Gerald Ford, Bill Clinton, and George H.W. Bush. As exciting as their visits were to the student body, there was one other UMD visitor who takes a back seat to no one - Rosa Parks received an honorary Doctorate of Law degree at the UMD 1991 spring commencement.

The Tavern #1: the Biergarten, 22184 Michigan Avenue (at Howard St.), Dearborn MI 48124; (313) 561-7711

Although the faded words, "the Aviator", is what you see on the side of the building facing Michigan Avenue (the pre-Biergarten name), you've come to the right place.

The Biergarten offers a fine place to kick-back after a day on the Rouge: well-priced good food in a great old-timey tavern atmosphere. Crack research team member Paul Draus proved that UMD profs know what they're talking about as his "shot 'n a beer" description was right on the money. The appeal of the Biergarten is universal: its 5 o'clock on a Tuesday afternoon and all bars stools were taken, with folks from tee shirts to suits settled in.

The definition of a biergarten is an outdoor tavern or an outdoor area adjoining a tavern where alcohol is served. Although the Biergarten, according to the Detroit News, was voted in 2002 to be "the best biergarten Michigan", our waiti Jess has worked here 10 years and doesn't recall any outdoor bar activity. Oh well, overthinking a happy place is a waste of time better spent enjoying a cold bottle of Pabst Blue Ribbon beer and a bar burger that cures the hunger created by a paddling afternoon.

Each ceiling tile is an advertisement for area businesses, like a table place mat in a small town restaurant Up North, but on a much larger scale. On a lower plain, the Biergarten has 10 beers on tap (always nice to have a canoe-shaped tapper, thank you Leinenkugel) and about another 50 brands of beers are available in bottles including the above mentioned PBRs. The pub has 7 TVs, 2 dart boards, a pool table, a fine juke box, and Tiger schedules are all over the walls – now THAT's some fine décor!

It's never too early to plan your next meal, so before you hop in the car for the ride home you may want to stop at Buddy's Pizza, right next door to the Biergarten. Some of the best pie I've ever had was at breakfast time.

Now, for those paddlers among you yearning for fancier surroundings...

The Tavern #2: Bailey's Tavern, SE corner Michigan & Mason

- 37 beers on tap, plus PBR tall boys, many bottled beers/liquor choices

- 30 big screen TVs

- 6 pool tables, ping pong table, giant Jenga, Foosball

- Bench seating & bar-stool height chairs throughout – one table/set of chairs may be lowered for special needs customers (call ahead)

- Open air seating area along Mason Street

- Lower level available for private parties or special events (St. Patty's Day, televised boxing matches)

- And, saving the best for last, Bailey's finest selling point is that they do have table-top shuffleboard

Oh where have you gone, Pelican Club?

Chapter Sources: Dave Norwood, Sally Petrella, Terry Bakewell, www.umdearborn.edu

Thunder Bay River / Alpena Community College

Degree of Paddling Difficulty: beginner (level 1 of 3)

Livery: Adventureland Sports, corner of Long Rapids & Chisholm, Alpena MI 49707, 989-255-7796; www.adventurelandsports.com.

River Quote: "Wrote a note said *be back in a minute*, bought a boat and I sailed off in it" – Zac Brown Band

Thunder Bay Soundtrack: Bayou Country – Gritz, Kilauea – the Volcanos, School Days – Stanley Clarke, Knee Deep – Zac Brown Band, Straight No Chaser – Alpena Community College Jazz Ensemble

Detroit Tigers radio affiliate: listen to WRGZ 96.7FM to follow the Tigers when paddling the Thunder Bay River near the Alpena Community College campus.

Directions to the launch site: US23 North through downtown Alpena, left on to Long Rapids Road, left on to Bagley Street, cross over river and the Sytek Park launch is on your left. Restrooms available.

Directions to the take-out: US23 North through downtown Alpena, just past N 14th Street you will cross over the river, pass the Alpena Regional Medical Center on your right, turn left at the next street, Long Rapids Road, and then immediately left into Duck Park. Restrooms available. The barrier-free launch deck has elevated aluminum bars and a transfer system to assist disabled paddlers.

Background of the Thunder Bay River:

The 75-mile long Thunder Bay River flows from west to east, its headwaters rising west of the town of Atlanta, from there meandering through the village of Hillman, and then on to the river mouth in Alpena's Thunder Bay (western-most Lake Huron). The western half of the watershed is home to Michigan's only known elk herd. Watershed recreational opportunities include canoeing, kayaking and other boating, hiking, biking, camping, hunting, fishing, golfing, skiing, and snowmobiling. Arguably, the river's most fascinating section is within the paddle outlined in this chapter, the Alpena Wildlife Sanctuary. The Sanctuary viewing includes deer, fish, swans, ducks, turtles, and many types of birds as you navigate around multiple islands, the base of two sand dunes, and by a covered bridge. The fishing in this stretch of Thunder Bay River includes smallmouth & largemouth bass and pike.

Working to protect the entire river is the Thunder Bay River Watershed Council. The Thunder Bay Watershed includes the counties of Alpena, Alcona, Montmorency, Oscoda, and Presque Isle. The council's stated mission is "to protect and enhance the benefits provided by the river, ensuring the water quality and quantity for fisheries, wildlife, recreation and aesthetic enjoyment, today and in the years to come. The council provides a forum for discussion of problems and issues affecting the management of this resource".

Another fine steward of Michigan's outdoors is the group known as Huron Pines, whose work goes beyond the Thunder Bay River and Watershed to include conserving the rivers, lakes, and forests throughout Northeast Michigan. Specific to Thunder Bay River, Huron Pines conducts an on-going program to check the spread of erosion and invasive species, in a cooperative effort with AmeriCorps, local businesses and residents to find solutions as problems arise. The Huron Pines website is www.huronpines.org.

Camping: Along the banks of the Thunder Bay River, at the 1 mile mark of the trip outlined in this chapter, is the Alpena County Fairgrounds Campgrounds. The Fairgrounds has two boat launches, the smaller one for canoes and kayaks is to the north of the big boat launch. 12 of the 69 camp sites are along the river, all sites have electricity, 35 are pull-through (i.e. you don't have to back your vehicle in or out), and a few have water. The campground has restrooms, showers, a dumping station, kid's park, and a bike path. The address is 625 South 11ᵗʰ Avenue, Alpena MI 49707, 989-356-1847; www.alpenacounty.org/fairgrounds.

Paddling the Thunder Bay River:

- Total trip 2.7 miles, 1 hour and 36 minutes (contact the livery for river trip options)

This is a gorgeous paddle through the 500 acres of the Alpena Wildlife Sanctuary. From the launch at Sytek Park to the take-out at Duck Park, the trip is beginner-friendly, never boring, full of wildlife and glistening waters. Beginning in water 8' deep and 80' wide at Sytek, you'll soon find yourself in water as shallow as 1' and as wide as 400'. Walking and biking glides along the riverside *Alpena Bi-Path*. The Bi-Path is a 14-mile long paved pathway running along both of the river's banks through Alpena's downtown, connecting the town's marina and parks. The paddle for this chapter was taken in April, when water levels were above average. 8 tributaries flowing into Thunder Bay River ensure that there is always plenty of water for a canoe or kayak.

.5 mile/20 minutes: arrive at a major river split, the first of many as Thunder Bay River breaks into a series of fingers wrapping around low islands within the Sanctuary. A large, beautiful mute swan floats nearby. Paddle to the right at the split where a buoy bobs to the left.

.7 mile/25 minutes: where steps are visible rising up the steep right bank to the Bi-Path, and the main body of the river continues straight-ahead, make a hard left through the 15' wide channel (where far in the distance are the white fences of Alpena's Fairgrounds).

Turtles rest everywhere. Once through the neck of the narrow channel, Thunder Bay River widens dramatically into a shallow bay, 2' deep on the average, and 400' wide with a wonderful variety of wildlife. Sightings included mute swans, muskrats, river otters, woodpeckers, geese, egrets, kingfishers and cormorants. Adventureland Sports owner Erin Riopelle identified for us a rare wildlife species known as *logodiles*, distant cousins of crocodiles, lurking below the river's surface that occasionally grab the bottom of your boat (for man-made mayhem).

Once in the big bay, the Fairgrounds parade straight ahead (to the east) and the traffic on Washington Street/M32 flows to the right (south). The Fairgrounds has two boat launches with the smaller one for canoes and kayaks to the north of the big boat launch, and camping sites (see "Camping" in an earlier section of this chapter). Deer run on distant banks.

1 mile/ 40 minutes: arrive at the banks of the Fairgrounds and turn left/north. The Sanctuary bird species abound including grebes, red-wing blackbirds, coots, eagles, and turkey vultures.

1.3 miles/47 minutes: you've cleared the north end of the Fairgrounds, turning left/ west to paddle through the narrow channel neck, surrounded by cattails on each side. Pass the white condos in the distance to the right/north and, right of the condos, Duck Park comes into view.

1.5 miles/55 minutes: once through the channel, turn right/north at buoy 4 and face the condos on Cow Island. The island is so named as it used to be a cow pasture back when a Fairgrounds' bull swam across the river to visit some of the heifers there. *Well, hell-o ladies...*

1.6 miles/1 hour: at Cow Island, turn right/NE at the A-frame home with a deck and a turret/ small silo above it. Although the river features occasional holes where it runs 10' deep, the average depth today is 2'.

1.8 miles/1 hour and 8 minutes: at the split in the river, take the right fork. The left fork takes you beneath a covered bridge.

2 miles/1 hour and 14 minutes: at the river split, paddle to the right around Island Park, home to Alpena's last Native American tribal chief, *Sah-gon-ah-ka-to* (i.e. "Thunder Cloud"), who passed at age 93 in 1869. Looking to the left/NE at the split, you see the take-out at Duck Park. Island Park has 4 different eco-systems: swamp, high grassland, forest, and sandy. Sea turtles lay their eggs in the sandy portion of Island Park. A 3/4–mile long walking trail surrounds the 14-acre island, also known as Sportsmen's Island – an island worth exploring!

2.4 miles/1 hour and 30 minutes: with the Duck Park take-out visible to your left/ NW, you've reached the SE tip of Island Park. Turn to the left just before the George Washington Bridge that crosses over US23. You will be paddling parallel to US23 towards the pedestrian bridge connecting the mainland and Island Park.

2.7 miles/1 hour and 36 minutes: you are in! just beyond the pedestrian bridge at the barrier-free ramp on the right shore.

Thunder Bay River Crack Research Team: Paul "Mister P" Pienta, Eric Long, Jenny Long, Erin Riopelle, Maggie and Doc

The College: Alpena Community College

665 Johnson St., Alpena MI 49707-1495, 989-356-9021; www.discover.alpenacc.edu.

Now *that's* a mascot: representing the Lumberjacks of Alpena Community College, standing 30' tall alongside the institute, is not just any old Paul Bunyan, this is *Kaiser Paul Bunyan*. This very unique Paul Bunyan was created in the early-60s from hoods and fenders of old, mostly Kaiser-brand (thus this Paul's name), automobiles that were found in Detroit-area salvage yards. This very nomadic Paul was originally built for a 1960s Gaylord "Paul Bunyan Gas and Eat" and when that establishment went out of business in the early-70s, Kaiser Paul moved to Gaylord's Native American museum until it closed in 1980. Moving a few minutes south to Grayling, Kaiser Paul stood outside of the AuSable-Manistee Realty Co. for 19 years until making his (hopefully) final move in 1999 to Alpena CC. With a 2014 sandblast and a fresh coat of paint, Kaiser Paul Bunyan is one sharp-lookin' mascot.

Alpena Community College began serving Northeast Michigan in 1952 by offering classes at Alpena High School. 23 students made up the first graduating class in June 1954. The campus that Alpena CC has called home since 1957 came about in large part through the generosity of inventor and philanthropist Jesse Besser. Jesse developed the hand tamp block machine, which allows concrete blocks to be manufactured in the field at construction sites. The invention was a boon to the construction industry, and the Besser Manufacturing Company was its dominant producer. Frank Lloyd Wright was a customer of the company, hiring Besser to create one-of-a-kind concrete blocks to use in Wright's buildings.

The current campus was created in 1957 from donations of 23 acres of land from Jesse Besser and another 14 acres from the City of Alpena and the Michigan Department of Conservation. Since then, another 700 acres donated by Jesse Besser have allowed the Community College to expand dramatically to today's institute. The campus offers two-year degrees, one-year certificates, customized corporate training, and community education to all of Northeast Michigan. Each semester ACC's enrollment of over 2,000 comes from diverse backgrounds, ages, and academic goals, drawn by small class sizes, affordable tuition, and the convenience of two campus locations and online courses. Alpena Community College provides an environment where students can work on a college degree, continuing education, or acquire specific skills in a wide number of vocational/technical fields, with the option of transferring completed courses to a four-year college. Members of the community that are not ACC students may participate in the college program, "Association of Lifelong Learning", which includes anything from lectures to manufacturing plant tours to hikes to forums to canoe trips to any new - or just plain fun - learning, idea, thought, or activity.

The Tavern: John A. Lau Saloon, 414 N. 2nd Avenue (and Fletcher Street), Alpena MI 49707; (989) 354-6898; www.johnalausaloon.com

In 1856, Alpena was founded under the name "Fremont", in honor of presidential candidate John C. Fremont, and renamed Alpena in 1859. By the 1890s, things were rip-roarin' in town with 28 saloons serving the thirsty, including the John A. Lau Saloon that opened in 1893 at 414 Dock Street, operating until closed in the early-1920s by the Feds during Prohibition. Alpena's "Old Town Project" brought Lau's back-to-life in the 2-block area once known as Dock Street, now 2nd Avenue, returning the saloon to its original 1893 location.

A visit to John A. Lau's, Alpena's oldest bar, is a fun trip back through time, from the moment you enter by grabbing the loggers' axe buried in the front door (now THAT's a door handle!) 'til visiting the biergarten out back that's decorated as a street in the wild west. The bar décor is late-1800s including the fabulous old time piano. Back in the day, the upstairs was a brothel and the private banquet room was a funeral parlor with a morgue in the basement. As you enter Lau's, the drawing of a fetching wench against the back bar wall entices you to belly up and stay awhile. The room to the left is where the original bar stood – its small back bar once stretched all the way to the front door.

John Lau's wife Anges is said to haunt the tavern, according to paranormal investigators from Grayling and the readings on their equipment. A saloon that even the dead don't want to leave – now that's impressive! Above a table in the left sitting area is a 12' long "loggers boom log", described as "a boom stick, long, flat timbers chained end-to-end, making a virtual sidewalk 2' or more in width on the surface of the water, that contained hundreds of floating logs down the river during a log drive in the 1800s".

The crack research team gave high praise for the "Blinkie Morgan" burger (done to perfection), home-made chips (instead of the fries), strawberry shake, pulled pork sandwich, and spinach artichoke dip with toast-like chips. Unexpected was the fine review by Mister P who said the "blue cheese bacon chips are great – and I hate blue cheese".

Blinkie Morgan, one of Alpena's rougher citizens and for whom the burger was named, was wanted in many parts of the country. Reputed to have ridden with Jesse James, he bludgeoned to death a Cleveland policeman and, in general, done bad as a way of life. Blinkie was finally caught and arrested, in his Alpena hideout, by Sheriff Charles Lynch, Jr., in 1887.

John A. Lau's has the feel of a tavern you're likely to spend a future afternoon at.

Chapter Sources: Erin Riopelle, Jobe at Lau's Saloon, "Experience Alpena" magazine, www.alpenacc.edu, www.findagrave.com, www.roadsideamerica.com.

Tittabawassee River / Northwood University

Degree of Paddling Difficulty: beginner (level 1 of 3)

Livery: Ike's Mobile Kayak, (989) 750-5251, www.ikeskayaks.com; Ike's also services the Pine (near Alma), the Chippewa, the Cedar, and the Kawkawlin rivers.

River Quote: "No man can ever step in the same river twice, for it is not the same river and he is not the same man" – Greek Philosopher Heraclitus

Bonus River Quote: "Showers are for people who don't drive with the windows down" – noted Milwaukee Philosopher William D. Meeker

Tittabawassee River Soundtrack: My Generation – the Who (Pete Townsend turned 70 the day of the Tittabawassee River paddle), Bridge of Sighs – Robin Trower, Mississippi River Blues – Big Bill Broonzy, Sixfour – Colieda (live at the Tridge), Soul Love – David Bowie

Detroit Tigers radio affiliate: listen to WSGW 790AM to follow the Tigers when paddling the Tittabawassee near the Northwood U campus.

Directions to the launch site: US10 west of Midland to exit 119/Stark Road, Stark south to W Wackerly Street and turn right/west, Wackerly west to E Saginaw Road and turn right/west. Take E Saginaw to E Wackerly Street and turn left/west to the Averill Preserve on your left. In the Preserve, walk your canoe or kayak 1/5th mile from E Wackerly to where the river meets Averill Creek. Launch into the creek's still waters, paddling 10' to the river. No restrooms.

Directions to the take-out: M20 to downtown Midland, turn left/south on to Ashman, follow Ashman for 1/5th of the mile to the access at the Tridge. The barrier-free launch deck has elevated aluminum bars and a transfer system to assist disabled paddlers. Restrooms available.

Background of the Tittabawassee River:

The Tittabawassee flows in a generally SE direction for 90 miles, from its headwaters at Secord Lake through Sanford and Midland until it empties into the Saginaw River in Saginaw. It is in Midland that the Tittabawassee absorbs the Chippewa River beneath the Tridge. 2 paddling hours upstream from the Tittabawassee/Chippewa merger is where the trip outlined in this chapter launches, at a place called the Averill Preserve. The 74-acre Averill Preserve is home to over a mile of trails for hiking and exploring nature. The Preserve's "Overlook" offers fantastic panoramic views of the Tittabawassee.

Another beautiful Tittabawassee River sight is the "Tridge", where this chapter's trip ends. The Tridge, a 3-legged wooden footbridge that spans the confluence of the Tittabawassee and the Chippewa rivers, is fantastic. As you walk past the Farmers Market and onto the Tridge, look to your right – the river flowing towards you on the right (north) is the Tittabawassee, the river flowing towards you on the left (south) is the Chippewa. Next to the Farmers Market is the eastern terminus of the Pere Marquette Rail Trail, aka the Midland to Clare Rail Trail, a 30-mile long hiking-running-biking trail that connects Midland in the east with Clare in the west. This rail trail is built upon an abandoned CSX railroad corridor that was once a part of the Pere Marquette-Flint Railroad, and includes spurs to the Chippewa Nature Center and Sanford Park.

Since 1996, an effective steward of the lands within the Tittabawassee River Watershed has been the Little Forks Conservancy. The LFC partners with watershed landowners to protect and preserve the area's natural features. The Conservancy website is www. littleforks.org.

Camping: 10 minutes northwest of the Tittabawassee River take-out in Midland, where Black Creek merges with Sanford Lake (part of the Tittabawassee River), is the Black Creek State Forest Campground. The 23-site campground (with vault toilets) is for tent or small trailer use, with 15 of the sites large enough for a 40' vehicle/trailer. Reservations are not accepted as the sites are on a first come/first serve basis. The campground is in the town of Sanford at the intersection of Saginaw Road and West River Road, phone 989-275-5151.

Paddling the Tittabawassee River:

Launch at Averill Preserve, where Averill Creek flows into the Tittabawassee River. This section of the river has an average width of 80' and a depth that varies from 6' to 15'. The late-May paddle for this chapter was at "normal" water levels. Even when the river is running lower than usual, there's always plenty of water to canoe or kayak the Tittabawassee.

- Total trip 8 miles, 2 hours and 8 minutes; for another Tittabawassee trip idea…

Livery owner (& crack research team member) Glenn Isenhart occasionally paddles an optional route: begin by paddling against the moderate current, departing from the Tridge and heading upstream to where Sturgeon Creek merges with the river, then turning for the downstream ride back to the Tridge, a paddle of 1 hour and 15 minutes (contact livery for longer trip options).

.4 mile/8 minutes: a creek merges left. Visible up the creek is the Little Forks Conservancy walkway. The left bank is approximately where the old logging community of Averill once sent their cut trees into the river for processing downstream at the log mills.

1.7 miles/31 minutes: among the white pines and hemlocks on the bluff above the right bank, where a creek flows into the river, a park bench beckons within the Riverview Natural Area. Bald eagles frequently fly along this riverbank.

2.3 miles/40 minutes: the first homes viewed on today's trip are beyond the left bank and along Tittabawassee River Road.

3.5 miles/1 hour: a creek merges right on a severe diagonal, with 2 homes behind it. A few feet downstream from the creek, a wide riverbank bald spot among the grass indicates a popular gathering location. Deer are running alongside the river as swallows fly among us.

4 miles/1 hour and 7 minutes: a cell tower looms on the right shore.

5.2 miles/1 hour and 25 minutes: to the left, a tunnel at the river's edge emerges below where Dublin Road ends at the river. You are now paddling alongside Northwood University campus property to the left. Prairie Creek merges at the right (south) bank.

6.1 miles/1 hour and 39 minutes: to the left and within the Northwood U. campus you see the Hach Student Activity Center. In two minutes, paddle below phone lines crossing overhead.

6.5 miles/1 hour and 44 minutes: the brick structure of an old water intake plant stands tall along the right bank. Two minutes downstream, a small gap in the long break wall on the left allows Sturgeon Creek, flowing from the north, to merge into the river.

If additional exploration sounds like fun, turn left up Sturgeon Creek. This takes you below a part of the Pere Marquette rail trail (the trail that begins near the Tridge) as the creek, full of turtles, begins to widen. Beyond the Tittabawassee's right bank is the Currie Golf Course.

6.8 miles/1 hour and 45 minutes: past the left bank white fence is an outdoor skating rink. 5 minutes downstream, a small rust colored pedestrian bridge crosses a left shore creek. Glenn tells us paddling up this narrow creek takes you to a peaceful little area full of deer and birds.

The Tittabawassee now passes by the baseball diamonds of Emerson Park along the left, home to the annual Lee "Ike" Isenhart-Lefty Bartos Fast Pitch Softball Tournament Classic.

7.5 miles/2 hours: pass beneath the red Currie Parkway Bridge and 3 docks closely aligned along the right bank, favorite fishing spots.

7.8 miles/2 hours and 5 minutes: paddle below the M20 Bridge. The Courthouse is to the left and the Tridge is very visible directly ahead. The peninsula on your right narrows quickly as the Chippewa River will soon be flowing into the Tittabawassee. "River Days", spanning two days each July, rocks this wonderfully situated piece of land between the two big rivers. Besides the music and the food, the festival provides entertainment, activities and fun for all ages.

8 miles/2 hours and 8 minutes: you are in! after paddling below the Tridge and exiting at the ramp on the left shore.

Tittabawassee River Crack Research Team: Glenn Isenhart, Steve Arnosky, JJ Johnson, Ashlyn Hill, Jay Arons, Doc

The College: Northwood University

4000 Whiting Drive, Midland MI 48640, 800-622-9000; www.northwood.edu

In 2007, shortly after graduating from Northwood University, 21-year old Jose Jono Jumamoy became the youngest person to ever be elected mayor in the Philippines.

Since its inception, Northwood University has never wavered from its mission: to develop the future leaders of a global, free-enterprise society. Founded by Dr. Arthur E. Turner and Dr. R. Gary Stauffer in 1959 as Northwood Institute, in its first two years the private not-for-profit school was located in a 19th century mansion in Alma, a town 45 minutes to the southwest of Midland. The Institute was moved to Midland in 1961.

To Turner & Stauffer, what differentiated Northwood Institute from more traditional colleges was "The Northwood Idea": they envisioned a new type of university... one where the teaching of state-of-the-art AND ethics-driven management was required in our free-enterprise society for every aspect of business, whether technical, manufacturing, marketing, or retail.

Northwood offers Bachelor of Business Administration degrees with majors in Accounting, Automotive Aftermarket Management, Automotive Marketing/ Management, Finance, Management Information Systems, Economics, Fashion Marketing/Management, Health Care Management, Hospitality Management, International Business, Marketing, Management, Operations & Supply Chain Management, and Sports and Entertainment Management.

The growth since the 1961 move to Midland has been remarkable...

- Northwood Institute expanded their academic curricula and became recognized in 1993 as the accredited Northwood University.

- The DeVos Graduate School of Management was added and expanded.

- The Northwood facility established in Texas serves students in the Southwest USA.

- Northwood's Adult Degree Program has students in 20 locations in 8 states.

- The University's International Program Centers teach in Switzerland, Malaysia, Sri Lanka, and mainland China.

In 1982, Dr. Turner and Dr. Stauffer turned over the reins to Dr. David E. Fry, who in turn passed the baton to Dr. Keith A. Pretty in 2006. As the school's name and its leaders changed, the Northwood mission to spread the gospel of state-of-the-art and ethics-driven management to students in Michigan and all across the globe remained the same.

The athletic teams at Division II Northwood University, known as the Timberwolves, participate in the GLIAC, acronym for the Great Lakes Intercollegiate Athletic Conference. The person most identified with Northwood athletics is Pat Riepma. Pat was at Northwood for 21 years, as both head football coach and athletic director. As head coach from 1993-2007, Pat led Northwood to three GLIAC championships, reached the NCAA Division II playoffs four times, and was named GLIAC coach of the year four times. Pat passed away in 2015, and overshadowing his athletic achievements was the large number of people who talked about how Riepma impacted their lives... eternally optimistic, gracious, humble, encouraging, compassionate, respectful, spiritual, full of love of God and His creations. Pat Riepma was a special person and the stories from the folks at, or associated with, Northwood University show they knew how fortunate they were that Pat Riepma touched their lives.

Good night Sleepie Tollie, wherever you may be.

The Tavern: Oscar's Bar and Grill, 140 E Main Street, Midland MI 48640; 989-837-8680; www.oscarsinline.com

What's better after a Tittabawassee Tuesday than $1 Taco Tuesdays at Oscar's? *Tittabawassee Taco Tuesday* just rolls off the tongue. Chicken or beef, soft or hard shell, Oscar's tacos come to your table at a great price for some good eatin'. At Oscar's, when the Pabst keg runs dry, they rotate in a Molson's keg, then back to Pabst, and so on... it reminds one of a sign recently seen: "Did your beer win a blue ribbon?" It's becoming extremely difficult to find any fault with this fine establishment.

Manager John kindly took some time out of what looked to be a hectic day, and shared some tavern background with us...

Although the bar has the warm feel and look of an old timey saloon a century old, Oscar's Bar and Grill has only been in business since 2000. The bar resides in a structure that used to be two businesses: a JC Penney and, on the corner of Main and McDonald Street, a bank. Trading a department store and a bank for a tavern like Oscar's is on par with trading Steve Demeter for Norm Cash – that's as good as a trade gets. Owner Jim Wiseman, previous to opening Oscar's, worked in both the restaurant and construction industries, and he put the twin experiences to good use: in his bar basement work shop, he has produced all of the tavern wood workings including the cool back bar, tables, and booth benches.

The post-paddling need for chow 'n grog was split between Oscar's Bar and another exceptional enterprise on the other side of Main Street, Pizza Sam's. As crack researcher and livery owner Glenn was returning to his hometown of Midland from living in California, what he wanted most (after a hug from Lori) was a pie from Pizza Sam's, at the corner of Main & Ashman. After a day on the Tittabawassee (or the Chippewa) River, you'll want a Pizza Sam's pizza pie, too. The crack researchers couldn't verbally express their admiration for Pizza Sam's 'cause the pizza was too good to stop eating and comment on, but their happy faces said it all. You might want to call ahead as soon as you're off the river to get Sam's goodness in you as quickly as possible.

Pizza Sam's is at 102 W Main Street, Midland MI; 989-631-1934; www.pizzasams.com

Chapter Sources: Glenn Isenhart, Steve Arnosky, www.northwood.edu, www.huronpines.org, Midland Daily News

Paddling & Camping Checklist

Plan thoroughly, but be prepared to follow the current

First aid kit Clothesline rope River shoes & dry shoes

Zip locks (large & small) Bug spray Baseball cap

2 sets of vehicle keys Toilet paper $$$ and wallet

Dry clothes Dry (waterproof) bags Food

Water Rain poncho Plastic drop cloths (for rain)

Trash bags Knife Bungee cords

Camera Sunglasses Sun block

Cooler & ice Towels

Add for overnights...

Tent Sleeping bag Blankets & pillows

Thermarest/air mattress Mattress pump Campsite chairs

Flashlights Forks/spoons/plates Can opener

Grill & grate Pots/pans/large spoon Fire starters & matches/lighters

Hand towels Reynolds wrap (for leftovers) Soap, toothpaste/toothbrush

Dish soap/scrub brush Frisbees Euchre decks

Nose strips (for snoring friends) Ear plugs (because of snoring friends)

About the Author

"Canoeing and Kayaking College Campuses in Michigan" is Doc Fletcher's 8th published book, the 6th one immersing readers in the special joy of paddling Michigan's rivers. Canoe 'n Kayak experiences across the Wolverine state were also documented in "Weekend Canoeing in Michigan", "Michigan Rivers Less Paddled", "Paddling Michigan's Hidden Beauty", "Michigan's Pere Marquette River: Paddling Through Its History", and "Paddling Michigan's Pine: Tales From the River".

Doc's published titles flow beyond Michigan's shores in "Canoeing and Kayaking Wisconsin", featuring wonderful Badger State river adventures, while "Paddling and Pastimes" introduces the intrigued to urban paddling adventures down 6 rivers through big cities in the Midwest along with shoreline visits to major league baseball parks near each of those rivers.

With his wife Maggie, Doc travels across Michigan sharing river adventures at libraries and nature centers. Their website is www. canoeingmichiganrivers.com